ACTS OF LOVE

FOR ROCHELLE

It took only one
of Eros' arrows
for this love to take.
Aiming the truly
feathered shaft, he laughed,
"For the long haul, kids,"
and let it fly home.
"You'll never forget,
though thousands will slip
and others may fade,
this bright day of days
that you caught my eye."

SAPPHO

(fl. 600 B.C.)

1

gold-crowned Aphrodite, if only
this winning lot could fall to me

2

Love rattled my mind,
like a mountain wind rushing through oak trees.

3

For sure, sweet mother, I can weave my web no more,
overcome by slender Aphrodite with passion for a boy.

4

and again Love, the limb-loosener, excites me,
that sweet-then-bitter, invincible critter

5

Throned in brilliance, deathless Aphrodite,
wile-weaving child of Zeus, I beg you,
my queen, do not inflict me further
with heartache,

but come here, if ever before
you heard my voice from afar,
and, disposed to leave your father's
golden house, came

with chariot yoked. And beautiful, swift
sparrows, wings awhir above the dark earth,
delivered you down from heaven
through midair

and quickly arrived. But you, O blessed one,
with a smile on your deathless face, asked me
so now what was the trouble and so now
why was I calling,

and what do I want more than anything
to befall my manic heart. So now whom
do I persuade to lead you back into her love?
Sappho, who's done you wrong?

For if she runs away, soon she'll give chase.
If she refuses gifts, then she'll make them.
If she does not love, soon she'll have to love,
even if unwilling.

Come to me again now, and release me
from bitter cares, and all that my heart longs
to fulfill, fulfill. And may you yourself
be my ally.

CONTENTS

INTRODUCTION

Wendy Doniger

The translator who hopes to carry ("-late") the reader over ("trans-") from one language to another can program his magic transporter room of poetry to beam him up, Scotty, in either direction. The outward-bound method, from the target language (English) to the source language (in this case, Greek), aims to transport a twenty-first-century American reader into the head of an ancient Greek, like one of those characters who enter other peoples' heads in Hollywood movies (*Big, Vice Versa, Prelude to a Kiss, Face/Off*). This method assumes that, with a bit of hard work, We R Greeks. To do it right, the reader really does need to learn Greek, and then, of course, has no need for a translation. To do it half right, the translator must teach the reader (in notes) a great deal more about the Greeks than the reader probably wants to know. At the very least, the reader must learn the complex meanings of certain key words (like *eros*, which both does and does not mean "love"; the Greeks had a *lot* of words for it) and, beyond that, the entire social system that nourished and/or stifled various forms of love and sex in that time and place. A culture's context provides the warp on which its poetry is woven. This method is daunting (remember all those things that went wrong in the transporter room . . .).

Dudley Fitts, who also translated parts of *The Palatine Anthology*, used the outward-bound method in *The Poem Itself* (edited with Stanley Burnshaw). This book attempted to lure the reader into the *lingua incognita* by providing the original text and a very literal translation heavily larded with notes, hoping that this crash course would enable the reader to go back to the original and read it. Fitts, who was one of my teachers at Harvard long ago, urged me to try to do the same thing with Sanskrit, with disastrous results; a typical compound, faithfully preserving the Sanskrit word order, came out: "western-mountain-setting-sun-rays-abandoned-closing-lotus-like face." I realized then that to the extent that this method works at all, it works only with languages with which the reader is vaguely familiar, which is, in the terms of this game, cheating. But the lack of a significant readership at home in that way with ancient Greek also stymies any plans to propagate Greek translations on a massive popular scale. So much for the "We R Greeks" experiment.

Translation in the other direction, the homeward-bound, "Greeks R Us" direction, from the source language (Greek) to the target language (English), requires a different sort of talent. It substitutes for the particularities of the culture of the original an assumption of certain universal human emotions that make culture largely irrelevant, so that translation consists of taking each image, each sentiment, in the original, plunging with it down to the molten core of the human heart, and carrying that core back up to the surface of the earth in another spot, our spot. This same assumption underlies Leonard Bernstein's staging of *Romeo and Juliet* in the slums of New York as *West Side Story*, or Akira Kurosawa's setting of *Macbeth* in medieval Japan as *Throne of Blood*. English masterpieces of this ilk include Chapman's Homer, FitzGerald's *Rubáiyát of Omar Khayyám*, and the King James Bible (which inspired Henry Higgins, the Sanskritist in George Bernard Shaw's *Pygmalion*, to complain that Eliza Doolittle was murdering English, the language "of Shakespeare and Milton and the Bible").

George Economou could certainly have moved us either outward- or homeward-bound to render *The Palatine Anthology* into English. Outward-bound, he is a seasoned scholar and prolific translator (of *Piers Plowman* and C. P. Cavafy, as well as Euripides) and the author of a terrific book on the goddess Natura in medieval literature, a book that is part of the scholarly canon on the canon of Western literature. And as for homeward-bound, his own renowned poetry in English is clear proof that he has a strong voice in which to make any other poet's words his own. *Acts of Love* combines the best of both worlds. The absence of a critical apparatus (Look, Ma, no footnotes) tells us that we R not the Greeks, while the presence of Greek names (Toto, I don't think we're in Kansas anymore) tells us that the Greeks R not simply us. This is an entirely new genre and a translation unlike any I've ever seen. It creates a new world, not just of language but of culture and of sexuality.

At first, it seems that we are in our own world, speaking our own language, our own dialect. The vivid language of these translations makes us feel as if we ourselves, in our own time and place, are experiencing what the authors of the Greek poems tell us they experienced. The sense of familiarity is created at first reading by American slang phrases.

Let her screw herself!

and feeling her up

put me and this divine boy on the same wavelength

I played around

I'm a goner

Wine always outs love

he tore off a piece

how stressed out his breathing was

This is old hat

switch the "th" in thighs to an "s"

"Well, looky here. Such daring. And all wined up!"

Sure, sure, shoot me

"Good buddy, do you work out the boys at night, too?"

I don't want it off the rack

I just should be so lucky

Let's drop our clothes, babe

below the neck, nada

in her prime time or over the hill

So what do I do? Split or stick around?

Those hoity-toity boys

really turns me on

I'm not into wine
but you can get me drunk

Another poem addresses "Dawn, love's enemy," and concludes:

But when I embraced my slender love, how quickly
you came and shed on me your Schadenfreude light.

There is a hilarious poem to "Mr. No-name," who "hung there like a dead man" when he should have been erect but, when he was done, kept

stretching like there's no tomorrow. . . . So go stretch

And a phrase no ancient Greek could have spoken:

about as much attention as Lake Michigan

Economou even evokes popular song lyrics:

She can't get no satisfaction

I belong to Daddy

Shine on, horny Moon, for all-night stands

And even a parody of Yeats' version of a Greek myth, here substituting Ganymede for Leda:

> Hey, eagle—when your feathered glory
> caught up that pretty boy, did he take on
> scratch marks from your claws before you let him drop?

In one place, Economou obligingly offers us two different translations of the same poem, the first without Americanisms and the second with them. The first one begins:

> Bring water, my boy, and bring wine,
> and bring me garlands of flowers.

And the other begins:

> Waiter, a double Jack Daniel's on the rocks, please,
> and a dozen Wellfleet oysters on the half shell.

The second version moves us two thousand years and a few thousand miles from the first.

Another factor in these poems that makes us Americans feel right at home in ancient Greece is the intense sexual frankness, which sneaks in on the coattails of a powerful poetic diction to make us think (wrongly), Hell, I could have said that. Such words and phrases, taken out of their poetic context, out of the melody and rhythm of the phrases in which they occur, are startling:

expensive fuck-boys

I shot my white-hot wad

she can flit around a worn-down peg

hide my hard-on

So step up you red-hot well-hung lovers

one of your stand-up guys

> my dick hangs between my thighs, useless

> O lovely butt,
> sweetly oiled up

But each time such a phrase makes us feel that we are still *chez nous*, living our own sex lives, we are jolted out of our complacency by the casual interjection of Greek names, which seem at first to be all that is left of the otherness of the alien culture and make the slang phrases suddenly seem not natural but all the more striking and compelling. Such as:

> wet my whistle with wine of Mytilene

> Pasiphile puts out

> Big Daddy Zeus

> Diokles
> raised up a lizard
> from the tub,
> a veritable *Aphrodite Rising*.

Or, on the subject of growing old (several of the poems, rather sad and/or cynical poems, are about aging):

> Soon we'll look like Hecuba and Priam making it.

Two lines, in two different poems, use an English phrase that conjures up not merely Greece but the world of Homer (more precisely, well-known English translations of Homer):

> Agathon's lizard was rosy-fingered
> just the other day, now it's rosy-armed

and, playing upon the same cliché:

> After having laid rosy-assed Doris

One poem makes a myth personal:

> Leda with nothing on, Zeus hidden in the swan. . . .
> If Zeus is a swan, then I'm a white duck.

Other phrases mix sexual slang and Greek references:

> I had a big thing for young Alkippe

> lovely Trojan foreplay

> like a Thracian or a Phrygian sucking his beer
> through a straw, she was bent over and working hard

> Or is it because you're named after Herakles,
> dirty girl, and think that kissing cock's heroic?

The shock of recognition does a double take, transporting us first away from Lake Michigan to "Herakles" and then back to Lake Michigan with "kissing cock." But "kissing cock" and other slang phrases of stark anatomical precision give another sort of jolt of their own, for although they are the real words that people actually use to describe sex, and might well use in bed, they are not the words that most readers would usually encounter in poetry or utter in literary company. These words, however, are here set in lines and stanzas that transform them into poetry, which we do not usually speak. Economou puts words in our mouths, words that both are and are not our own words. The effect is to transform us into better versions of ourselves, to make us people simultaneously far more frank and far more articulate than we really are. This is a magical world in which, when we speak, our words are perfect.

It takes very good poetry indeed to achieve this kind of musical, evocative intensity, which is what we encounter in *Acts of Love*. There are wonderful internal rhymes ("that sweet-then-bitter, invincible critter") and the occasional end rhyme:

> Love customized her fingernails with his sly art,
> so Heliodora's scratchies go straight to the heart.

But even without these formal elements, every poem is made of good, sweet lines of verbal music that make the rough words seem just right, absolving us of obscenity. As W. H. Auden said in his poem on the death of Yeats, time that

> will pardon Paul Claudel,
> Pardons him for writing well.

The poems are more about sex than about love, and, like sex, some of them are dirty, many are very funny, most are charmingly witty, and a few (about the sex lives of men and, occasionally, women as they age) are quite sad.

As I came to realize when I translated the Sanskrit *Kamasutra*, English lacks a register corresponding to the matter-of-fact terminology of the Sanskrit text, a register midway between the obscene and the medical. The obscene will jar the English-speaking reader in an inappropriate way, and in any case, in this post-rap-and-David-Mamet age, the people who do use the word "fuck" seldom use it to designate the sexual act. The medical is equally inappropriate. The only English register I felt I could use was the literary, which works best by avoiding the actual words altogether and creating effects by indirection, nuance, suggestion. Economou, however, calls a spade a spade, and gets away with it because of the power and immediacy of the language and the intimacy of the diction. The result is extraordinarily erotic.

Moreover, these poems transform not only our language but our mind-set, making us unconsciously identify with people who are either more promiscuous or more open about their promiscuity than most of us are, thus luring us out of our own judgmental minds. As with our crude sexual language, so with our crude sexual mores we ricochet from sentimental, sanctimonious chastity to out-of-control sexual gratification. But Economou has created a world not only of linguistic sexual freedom, a world in which one can say ("can" in the sense both of permission and of ability) anything, but of imagined total social-sexual freedom, a magical world in which I can fuck anyone I want, in any way I want. In these poems, anything goes: the seduction of very young boys, the casual switching from boys to women or the other way ("I've switched from boys' toys to the girls' "), flipping women over to pretend that they're boys and using them that way (also a popular trope in the *Arabian Nights*). This is a world where sex has no consequences—not just no AIDS, but no pregnancy (one woman is already pregnant when the poet has her, and another is rumored to be "knocked up," but no pregnancy lurks in anyone's future), no custody fights, no duels at dawn, just an occasional bit of piquant jealousy when one is caught in flagrant delight (which is what I used to think "in flagrante delicto" meant, an early translation error). Older men, older women, very young boys, anything that moves—the only people who seem to be sexually out of bounds, or, rather, sexually uninteresting, are very young girls.

The voices in these poems are not the voices of a Greek Oscar Wilde or Tallulah Bankhead making witty, sexually frank statements calculated to *épater les bourgeois*. On the contrary, the poet assumes that he is speaking to a company of like-minded sensualists who share his sexual freedom. It is not simply the absence of AIDS or the moral majority that marks this world apart from the bathhouses of San Francisco in the 1960s but the absence of the slightest hint of censure from society as a whole, and therefore of the need either to lie to or to defy that society. It's not a matter of Greeks being freer than we are; surely they had their hang-ups, as all societies do, though the liberating thing for us is that they had *different* hang-ups from ours. No, in Economou's translations, *all* cultural chains are broken, both Greek and American; the voices in his poems seem to be cut loose from the moorings of their own culture (as well of ours, of course).

That the sexual diction that seems at first to tie us to our own time and place eventually transcends those bounds and creates a world that is neither Greece nor America is another amazing achievement of these poems. We are left in a no-man's-land, and this is one of the things that makes these poems so incredibly sexy. Economou catapults us into a world of joyous, honest, rampant bisexuality, a world every bit as fantastic as that of Tolkien or George Lucas, but a lot more fun. And this one is for grown-ups.

———

WENDY DONIGER graduated from Radcliffe College and received her Ph.D. from Harvard University and her D.Phil. from Oxford University. She is the Mircea Eliade Distinguished Service Professor of the History of Religions at the University of Chicago and the author of many books, most recently *The Bedtrick: Tales of Sex and Masquerade* and *The Woman Who Pretended to Be Who She Was.*

TRANSLATOR'S PREFACE

No problem is as consubstantial to literature and its modest
mystery as the one posed by translation.

—JORGE LUIS BORGES

The Greek Anthology, a monumental compilation of more than four
thousand short poems, which the Greeks called *epigrammata*, has come
down to us through a unique history of transmissions and transforma-
tions. The singular version known as *The Palatine Anthology* was discov-
ered by the French humanist Salmasius in the library of the Count of
Palatine at Heidelberg in 1606, after having disappeared for perhaps
as many as three centuries. Authorities generally agree that the Palatine
collection was based on the definitive Byzantine anthology of classical
epigrams made by Konstantinos Kephalas in the early tenth century.
Kephalas' anthology was the source as well of the redaction of it made
by the learned Byzantine monk Maximus Planudes (ca. 1255–1305),
which was first printed in 1484. But in his anthology, which apparently
replaced the Palatine version of Kephalas in the interim, Planudes
made numerous changes in the form of many omissions and some
additions, the latter being an entire book of epigrams on the subject
of works of art, which was probably derived from a lost book in the
anthology of Kephalas. Together, the fifteen books of *The Palatine An-
thology* and this valuable preservation of poems known as "the
Planudean Appendix," added as Book 16, constitute the work to which
we now refer as *The Greek Anthology*.

The foundations of this great medieval collection were laid centuries before, during the Hellenistic and early Byzantine eras. The major sources used by Kephalas were the three anthologies (the Greek word *anthologia* means "gathering of flowers") made by Meleagros in the first century B.C., by Philippos of Thessalonika in the first century A.D., and by Agathias Scholastikos in the sixth century A.D., during the reign of Justinian. Of these, the *Stephanos* ("the Garland") put together by Meleagros is the most important. Assembling approximately a thousand poems on several themes dating from the seventh to the third century but not including any poems other than his own from his own time, Meleagros arranged the works of his contributors partially in groupings but mainly in alphabetical order according to the first letters of the poems. In his versified proem, he mentions forty-seven poets, associating each with a specific flower; hence the concept of gathering poets into a garland or wreath. Although he included Anakreon, Archilochos, and Sappho, none of the selections from these three poets, some of which are of doubtful ascription, are suited to the amatory theme of this collection. Thus, I have included work outside of *The Greek Anthology* by these three poets at the beginning of this "garland," choosing selections that deal with the subject of love even if they are not epigrams in form. Philippos says in his proem, also in verse, that his garland is made in imitation of Meleagros'; he names thirteen poets with their personal flowers but leaves it to his readers to match the others with whatever freshly blooming flowers they like. None of the eighty-nine poems of his own that Philippos contributed to his garland is a love poem, however. Like his predecessors, Agathias included in his *Cycle* poems of his own among his wide selection of works by contemporaries who, like him, sought to emulate the language as well as the themes of their ancient models.

In the course of its transformation from ancient papyrus scrolls to medieval codex, culminating in the Kephalas compilation, the *Anthology* absorbed poems from a number of other sources, the most important of which are the anthologies of love poems made by Rufinus and Straton. Following the example of Agathias, who says in his prose proem that he classified the poems in his *Cycle* thematically, Kephalas made a radical rearrangement of the large number of poems at his disposal into books under such subject-matter headings as dedicatory, sympotic, erotic, hortatory and admonitory, epideictic, and ecphrastic, and included many epigrams on various Christian topics. Two of the most significant decisions the Byzantine anthologist made were to add about a hundred amatory epigrams collected by Rufinus to those from his three major sources to create Book 5, "Epigrammata Erotica," and to combine a collection of pederastic poems composed by Straton with other epigrams on homosexual themes in his sources (a redistribution process that was not without its faults) to create Book 12, the collection of homoerotic poems called "Mousa Paidike." Thus, Kephalas managed to preserve some 567 epigrams on the subject of love, a notably rich and diverse contribution to the poetic legacy of the ancient world to posterity.[1]

A unique, wide-ranging, and highly versatile form, the Greek epigram originated as an inscription upon an object to indicate who made it, who was buried under it, or to whom it was dedicated. Though the form's reach gradually and ultimately extended well beyond its earlier functions and provided a flexible medium for the expression of subjective concerns, the epigram retained its signature meter, the elegiac couplet, a line in hexameter followed by one in pentameter, to put it simply.[2] By the late fourth and early third century B.C., it had begun to develop into a distinctive kind of poem, usually in the form of a couplet or quatrain, but often as long as six or eight lines, that was characterized by its pithiness and personal tone. The more it was used the more it gained in currency, and the Hellenistic poets fully explored the limits of its possibilities. Of all the subjects addressed in the epigram, none has proven more amenable to its poetic properties and potentialities than the works of golden Aphrodite and her son winged Eros.

While there have been fine translations of some of these amatory epigrams, they have also been subjected to a series of translation practices that have distorted or suppressed an important aspect of their linguistic and aesthetic integrity. Too often, readers have encountered these poems in English versions that have Latinized or sanitized their discourse in Greek through euphemism, circumlocution, or downright bowdlerization. Such strategies obstruct the flow of the poem's sense from one language into the other in fundamental ways; so, too, in more sophisticated and seductive ways, do the cries of "Look at me!" from translators who have been tempted to favor the sight and sound of their own ingenuities over the exigencies of the poem they are translating. Just as I have committed myself to eliminating the former obstacle, I also hope I have avoided the vanity of the latter. Still, I would affirm the value, on a relative scale to be sure, of all translations and support the defense of the enterprise against "the superstition about the inferiority of translations" that Borges eloquently made in the essay from which the above epigraph has been quoted.[3]

Just as Borges sees through the "absentmindedness" of the well-known Italian pairing of *traditore* and *traduttore* ("traitor" and "translator"), to which he alludes in the same essay, I would disagree with Robert Frost's famous quip that "poetry is what gets lost in translation." Poetry, even if and by necessity of a different nature, can be won through translation. Much depends upon the translator to achieve a comparable level of performance. In making these translations, I have used both closed and open forms, but I have also attempted to introduce the prose poem as an effective vehicle for some epigrams that run from eight lines to longer and that seem to flirt with a narrative, even anecdotal, end.

Like many other translators and scholars in recent years, I have chosen to follow the practice of using English transliteration rather than the once ubiquitous Latinized spellings of Greek names and words, although I do so without a compulsion for consistency. I prefer Meleagros to Meleager, Alkaios to Alcaeus, but allow Plato and Bacchus to stand, just as in the notes I will refer to C. P. Cavafy by the name the English-speaking world knows him by rather than the Greek Kaváfis.

I have also chosen to order the presentation of the poets in this collection in six groupings, in the interests of chronological clarity and coherence. After the three earlier poets, Anakreon, Archilochos, and Sappho, I have arranged the poets from *The Greek Anthology* under the headings "From *The Garland of Meleagros*," "From *The Garland of Philippos of Thessalonika*," "From *The Cycle of Agathias Scholastikos*," "Other Poets in *The Greek Anthology*," and "Anonymous Poems."

Finally, I would like to thank John Ganim for thinking of me in the first place, Will Murphy of Random House for helping me discover and define this project, and Evelyn O'Hara, who played a critical role in the early stages of this work's preparation for publication. Julia Cheiffetz, my editor at Random House, has given me unusual support and assistance, and I have benefited considerably from her unerring literary judgment and critical acumen. I want to thank David Ninemire and Diane Lisco of the Philadelphia City Institute Branch of our great Free Library for their expert assistance in putting some essential books into my hands. Stavros Deligiorgis and Vassilis Lambropoulos always had the right advice to give when asked for some. I am also grateful to my sister, Georgia Economou, Nicholas Howe and Robert W. Hanning, and my agents, Ann and Donald Farber, for their generous encouragement. Rochelle Owens and William R. Askins did me the special favor of reading all of these translations, a good number of which are the better for it.

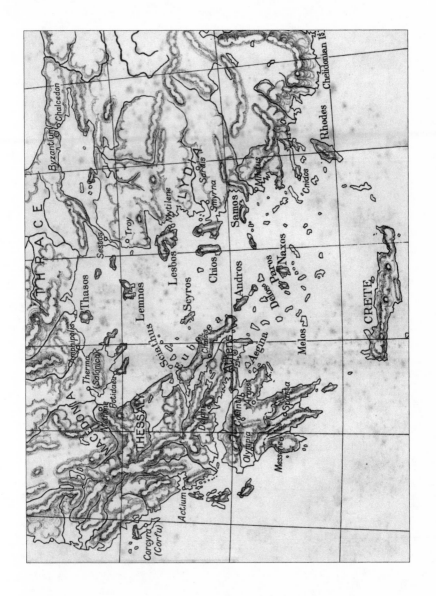

THRACE

Byzantium ○ Chalcedon

Sestos

Troy ○

LYDIA

Smyrna ○ ○ Sardis

Mytilene

Lesbos

Chios

Samos

Miletus

Cnidos

Rhodes

Chelidonian Is.

MACEDONIA

Therma
(Salonica)

Amphipolis

Thasos

Methone ○
Potidaea

THESSALY

Lemnos

Sciathus

Scyros

Andros

Delos Paros

Naxos

CRETE

Euboea

Chalcis

Delphi

Athens

Aegina

Corinth
Argos

Olympia

Messene ○

Sparta

Melos

Actium

Corcyra
(Corfu)

ACTS OF LOVE

ANAKREON

(ca. 563–478 B.C.)

1

Lord Loud-Shout, playmate
to Love the Winner,
and the dark-eyed Nymphs
and rosy Aphrodite,
roaming the hilltops,
I will kneel to you
that you come to me
disposed to answer
my prayer favorably,
O, D I O N Y S O S,
and advise Kleoboulos
to accept my love.

2

I've got a crush on Kleoboulos,
I'm crazy about Kleoboulos,
can't take my eyes off Kleoboulos.

3

Say, boy, you with that girlish look,
I'm after you and you don't care,
don't even know you're my charioteer
and hold the reins to my heart and soul.

4

Look how I climb up the White Cliff,
drunk with love, to dive into churning waters.

5

Since you're so open to strangers,
how about a little drink for me.

6

See how Love, like a blacksmith, hammers me,
and then douses me in the chilly stream.

7

Bring water, my boy, and bring wine,
and bring me garlands of flowers.
I'm ready for another bout with Love.

> (*or*)

Waiter, a double Jack Daniel's on the rocks, please,
and a dozen Wellfleet oysters on the half shell.
I'm here to take on Love's next challenger.

> (*or*)

Cheers!
    Light me!
        Ring the bell!

8

        ... and it was in this room
he played at marriage but not as the married man.

9

So why do you look askance at me, my Thracian filly, and shy away
from me as if I have no idea what I'm doing? You should know I could
bridle you like that, mount and ride you around this track. For the mo-
ment, you enjoy the pleasures of the meadow, to frolic, frisk, and
graze, believing there's no rider around who can break you.

10

It seems I'm both in love and not in love,
mad about somebody, and yet not mad.

11

Golden-haired Love hits me
                          with his purple ball,
inviting me to play
                  with the girl in the smart sandals.
But no,
         she comes from that fine place,
                        Lesbos,
is turned off
         by my white hairs
and goes all agape
              after someone else.

12

I fly up on light wings
                  to fetch Love from Olympos,
but he won't play anymore
                    now my beard's getting gray,
but flies right past me,
blown aside by the wake
               of his glittering wings.

ARCHILOCHOS

(fl. 648 B.C.)

1

she delighted in holding a myrtle branch
and a lovely rosebush flower...
                              ...and her hair's
shadow fell over her shoulders and back

2

for such a hankering to love cut loose under my heart,
poured a heavy mist over my eyes,
stole my dim wits clean out of me

3

but, my friend, desire, the limb-loosener, takes me down

4

As a fig tree in rocky soil feeds many crows,
so amenable Pasiphile puts out for strangers.

5

like a Thracian or a Phrygian sucking his beer
through a straw, she was bent over and working hard

6

"...refraining altogether.
Dare a mutual...

But if you're fully heated up from the heart down,
there's someone at our place
who has a yen for you,

a lovely young thing. To me she looks
like your perfect 'ten,'
and you can make her yours."

So she said. And so I replied:
"Daughter of Amphimedo,
that fine and sober

lady now in the moldering earth's embrace,
the pleasures love's goddess gives
to us young men are many

besides the holy deed; one of these will do.
But such matters, at our leisure,
after darkness falls,

we two can talk over as the gods listen.
I'll be good, just as you ask,
though mightily turned on.

But to slip under your fence up to the gate,
don't deny me that, hon,
for I'll walk on the grass

but not, I promise, into the garden. As for
Neoboule, some other guy can have her.
Hey, she's overripe and twice your age,

and her girlhood flower's bloom is long gone,
with any charm she might have had.
She can't get no satisfaction,

that sex-mad female run amok.
Let her screw herself!
And God forbid

I have a wife like her, for my neighbors
to get a big laugh out of.
I'd much prefer you,

who are neither faithless nor two-faced,
while she's so eager
to take on all comers.

I'm scared to death I'd get blind preemies
on her—if I come on too strong—
just like the proverb's bitch."

Enough said. I take the girl by the hand
and lay her down on a bed
of flowers, covering her

with my soft cloak, my arm beneath her neck.
That wide-eyed look of a fawn
I relieve her of kindly,

and gently take her breasts in hand,
moving her to show her sweet self,
her enchanting young flesh,

and feeling her up all over her lovely body,
I shot my white-hot wad
while petting her light brown hair.

FROM
THE GREEK
ANTHOLOGY

FROM
THE GARLAND OF MELEAGROS

ALKAIOS

(fl. 190 B.C.)

1

I hate Love. Why doesn't his heaviness hunt
wild beasts instead of shooting at my heart?
What's in it for a god to burn up a man?
Or what kind of trophy would my head make?

2

Your leg's getting hairy, Nikandros. Watch your ass,
lest it do the same without your knowing.
Then you'll see a scarcity of lovers. For now,
reflect upon youth irrevocable.

3

Zeus, under the steep hill of Olympia
crown Peithenor, Aphrodite's second son.
I beg you, don't turn eagle and carry him off
as cupbearer replacement for that Trojan boy.
If you hold dear any gift of mine from the Muses,
put me and this divine boy on the same wavelength.

ASKLEPIADES

(fl. 290 B.C.)

1

Didi waves her wand—and man—takes full command
of me, and I melt like wax just by taking her in.
What do I care if she's dark? So is charcoal.
When we fire it, it glows like a bed of roses.

2

Good lamp, three times before you Heraklea swore
to come and didn't. Lamp, if you're divine,
pay back that cheat. When she's at home fooling around
with a friend, go out, leave them in the dark.

3

Snow, hail, darken, lighten, thunder, and shake,
shake out all your black clouds onto the ground!
Kill me and I'll stop, let me live and I'll
go through worse to make music at her door.
For the same god who masters me masters you Zeus,
who, turned to gold at his call, pierced the bronze chamber.

4

What good's your long-preserved virginity?
In Hades, my girl, none do there embrace.
The joys of Love belong between the gates of life,
but we lie below, dear virgin, as dust and bone.

5

Stay up here
              my wreaths
                      where I hang you
on the door,
             don't be eager
                     to shake your leaves,
for I've watered you
             with my tears
                    (rainy-eyed lover).
But when the door opens
             and you see him,
                         shower
his head
         with my rain,
              that at least
my beloved's fair hair
             may drink up my tears.

6

With her sweet, yearning face moist with desire,
lovely Nikarete appeared in her high window,
dear Goddess, and seeing Kleophon at her door,
with his dazzling sweet blue eyes, was blown away.

7

O queen of Paphos, once I played around
with the winning Hermione, whose belt,
many colored, gold lettered, read in its circuit,
"Love me and don't be sad I'm another's."

8

Viperish Philainion has stung me.
No bite marks, but it hurts down to the fingertips.
Well, Loves, I'm a goner. Half-asleep I trod on
a whore—just a brush, I know, but it's death.

9

Sweet in summer
to a thirsty man
is a drink of snow.
Sweet to sailors
after wintry weather
to feel spring's Zephyr.
But sweeter's still
the praise of Kypris
by two lovers
under a shared cloak.

10

Demetrios, go to the market and get three small herrings from Amyn-
tos, ten smelts, and two dozen nice shrimp (he'll count them out for
you) and come right back home with them. And while you're at it, get
six rose wreaths from Thauborios—and, since it's on your way, might
as well drop in on Tryphera and invite her over.

11

A long winter night, the Pleiads are halfway up,
and I, soaking wet, keep showing up at her door,
smitten by desire for this cheat. This can't be love,
Goddess, but some kind of flaming-arrow torture.

12

Goddess, to you Lysidike dedicated
her riding spur, golden goad of her gorgeous leg,
with which she worked out many horsies on their backs,

never reddening her own thighs, so lightly she rocked.
No spur needed for her to cross the finish line,
wherefore she hung her golden weapon on your gate.

13

Bitto and Nannion, the Samians, refuse to cruise
at Aphrodite's place as she ordains,
but desert to other not so good practices.
Goddess, hate these renegades to your bed.

14

Not quite twenty-two and life's a burden.
You Loves, what's this mistreatment? Why burn me?
If something happens to me, what'll you do?
Play dice as before, that's what, you dummies!

15

Drink up, Asklepiades. Why the tears? What's your problem? You're
not the only one the merciless Goddess has captured, not the only one
for whom bitter Love tightens his bow and sharpens his arrows. Why
lie in the dust when you're still alive? Let's have a drink of Bacchus,
strong and neat. The light of day is but a finger long. Shall we just wait
around to follow the lamp to bed? Let's have a drink, sad lover. It won't
be long now, my black-and-blue friend, that we shall take the big
sleep.

16

With wings on your back, bow and arrows in your hand,
you'll be described as Aphrodite's boy, not Love.

17

I'm just a little Love
far away from his mother,
still easy to catch,
but from Damis' house
I don't fly high or far.

With him I'm loving and loved,
without competition
or a care for the many,
but well-matched with one.

18

Wine always outs love.

                  Nick denied it

but his toasts

            betrayed him.

For sure, he shed tears,

                looked at the floor,

had that hangdog look,

            and his wreath,

tied tight on his head,

            wouldn't stay in place.

19

Not yet big enough to carry a bow or to act tough,
my baby Love, gold tablet in hand, returns to Mama,
and reads with a lisp the recipes for love spells
that Philokrates put on Antigenes' soul.

20

Loves, what little is left of my soul, leave it alone, such as it is, and give it a rest for god's sake. Or else stop shooting me with arrows but hit me with thunderstrikes, yes, reduce me utterly to ashes and cinder. Yes, yes, hit me, Loves, for worn out as I am by my troubles, I'd like to have just this one wish from you.

DIOSKORIDES

(late third, early second centuries B.C.)

1

Dear Adonis
winning Aristonoe
wounded me
when she tore
at her breasts
by your bier.
If she'll do me
the same honor
when I die
take me along
—no excuses—
as a shipmate
on your voyage.

2

When moved to make love to your pregnant wife,
never bed her down face to face. For then
you'll be riding a big wave, a bit frustrated
trying to row her, being tossed and rolled yourself.
Instead, turn her over and make merry
with her rosy butt, instructing her in boy love.

3

After having laid rosy-assed Doris,
I felt immortal amidst green pastures.

For, having wrapped those gorgeous legs around my waist,
she methodically finished off Love's long course,
fixing me with those glassy eyes, which she fluttered
like leaves caught in a breeze, as she thrust back and forth,
till we both came mightily together,
and Doris just lay there, spent and slack-limbed.

4

They drive me crazy, those rose-red bubbling lips, the doors to that
heavenly-tasting mouth that melts my soul, and eyes that flash be-
neath thick eyebrows, the nets and snares of my innermost man, and
those juicy breasts, perfectly formed and matched, utterly charming
and better than any flower. But why preach to the choir? The reeds of
Midas bear witness to the fate of babblers.

5

If little Demophilos kisses his lovers
when he's fully matured as he kisses me now
as a child, O Aphrodite, his mother's door
shall simply never have a moment's peace at night.

6

Love, bane of men, molded Sosarchos' ass
soft as marrow just for the fun of it,
to annoy Zeus now, because those two thighs
have so much more honey than Ganymede's.

7

When you look at Hermogenes, that vulture-boy, be sure you have
plenty of cash in hand, and maybe you'll fulfill your heart's desire and
wipe that scowl off his face. But cast your hooked line into the harbor
without bait and you'll pull nothing but water. Remember, expensive
fuck-boys know neither shame nor pity.

8

I now call to witness
the very powers of friendship
by which he first swore,
that honey-faced Athenaios.

HEDYLOS

(fl. 280 B.C.)

1

Wine and wily "Cheers" and Nick's
sweet lovin' put Aggie straight to sleep;
her maidenly passion's spoils lie still be-
fore Love's Goddess, all of them wet with her scent,
her sandals and the soft top that fits round her titties,
sole witnesses to how she slept as he tore off a piece.

2

Bacchus and Aphrodite, limb-looseners both,
have just had a daughter, limb-loosener gout.

KALLIMACHOS

(310–ca. 240 B.C.)

1

I loathe the serial poem, rejoice not
in a road that many people travel,
and hate a beloved who's made the rounds.
No fountain drinks, things public disgust me.
But you, Lysanias, I thought fair, I thought fine.
No sooner said than Echo replies, "But not mine."

2

Kleon of Thessaly, you poor, poor, thing!
By the dazzling sun, I didn't know you.
Where've you been, pathetic bag of hair and bones?
Have you caught my luck, been hit hard by heaven?
Now I get it. Euxitheos took off with you.
When you came here, you just ate him up with both eyes.

3

But half my soul still breathes, the other half
off with Love or Death, don't know, but it's gone.
With one of the boys again? I often said,
"Don't take him in, young men, that runaway."
Look for it at . . . for someplace around there
that lovelorn condemned thing is hanging out.

4

Your hunter in the hills, Epikydes, tracks every hare
and the slot of every hind through frost and snow.
Show him a wounded beast, and he won't take it.

That's my way of loving: to pursue my quarry
as it runs away, and to fly right by
whatever lies in my path for the taking.

5

If I came to you in fun on purpose, Archinos, then a thousand apologies, but if I'm here strictly because I couldn't help myself, consider the urgency of it. Strong wine and Love compelled me. One pulled me while the other took away my sobriety. But when I came, I didn't howl about who I was or whose, but kissed the doorpost. If that's a sin, then I'm a sinner.

6

I swear it by the gods, there is
fire hidden under these embers.
I can't trust myself. Don't hold me.
Still waters can gnaw away at a wall.
I fear, my friend, lest the silent
creeper chase me back into love.

7

Menippos, I know that I'm not wealthy,
but, for god's sake, please stop telling me so.
To hear incessant bitter words pains me.
Yes, dear, this is your most unlovely side.

8

On the twentieth of last month, I said,
"I'll get you, Menekrates, no escape."
Today, the tenth, the ox accepts the yoke
in just twenty days. Good for Hermes! Good for me!

9

What an excellent charm for the lovelorn Polyphemos found! You can bet he wasn't completely unschooled, that Cyclops. The Muses make Love very thin, Philip, and learning is a kind of panacea for every ill.

And I think hunger has one good to set against its evils, the radical excision of the boy-love disease. I certainly have my reasons for telling Love, "Your wings are being clipped, little guy. I'm not in the least afraid of you." For I have at home both of the charms that will treat this grave wound.

10

If handsome, dark Theokritos hate me, hate him
back times four, but if he love me, love him.
For surely, divine Zeus, by fair-haired Ganymede,
you were in love once, too. That's enough said.

11

We hadn't noticed our guest is wounded.
You saw, though, how stressed out his breathing was
when he took his third drink. And how the roses
shed their petals and fell from his wreath to the ground.
He's on fire. By god, I'm not just guessing,
but being a thief myself, I read the clues.

12

Kallignotos swore to Ionis that no man
or other woman would be dearer to him.
He swore, but it's true what they say about lovers'
oaths, that they never get past the gods' ears.
Now he's on fire for some boy and the poor girl,
like a ghost town, gets no account or word.

13

May such a sleep be yours, Konopion,
as that you make me take by your cold doors.
May such a sleep as that your lover sleeps
be yours, bitch. You've not a dream of pity.
Neighbors show pity, but you, not a dream.
May white hair remind you of this—and soon!

MELEAGROS

(ca. 140–ca. 70 B.C.)

1

Sacred Night and Lamp, you and you alone we chose,
both of us, to be the confidants of our oaths.
He pledged his affection and I never to leave,
to which you bore common witness. But now, alas,
he maintains these oaths were made in running water,
and you, Lamp, see him snugly in another's arms.

2

Flee! My soul warns me against Heliodora's love,
for it knows all about past jealousies and tears.
It's an order, but I've no strength, and my soul still
loves the girl even as it keeps on warning me.

3

Just keep burning my scorched soul, nasty Love,
she'll fly away. She has wings, too, you know.

4

Timarion, your kiss is glue, your eyes are flames.
If you look at me, I'm burnt, kiss me and I'm stuck.

5

Fill my cup and just keep saying, "Heliodora's."
Say it again, mingling the wine with that sweet name.
Let me wear that wreath, though last night's, drenched with her
    scent,

to remember her by. And now look at that rose,
the one friendly to Love, how it's covered with tears
because she's elsewhere, not here in my arms.

6

How sweet the music
                    you make on the lyre
Arcadian Pan would know—
                         yes, Pan knows,
you have the right touch,
                   Zenophila.
So how do I escape you?
                  The Loves have me
surrounded
                and don't give me a chance to
catch my breath,
              for Beauty, or the Muse
or one of the Graces
                throws this desire my way—
what can I say?
              I'm just burning up.

7

By God, I'd rather hear Heliodora whisper
sweet nothings in my ear than Apollo's harp.

8

The flowers in the wreath that crowns Heliodora
are fading, but she outshines that wreath and crowns it.

9

Now the white violet blooms,
the rain-loving narcissus blooms,
the lilies of the hilly fields bloom,
and now love's darling, the flower

of all spring's flowers, sweet rose of Persuasion,
Zenophila, blooms.
So why do you laugh so vainly,
meadows, over your lustrous tresses?
This girl is better than any garland.

10

Who introduced loquacious Zenophila to me?
Who brought me one of the Graces as my mistress?
That man did a gracious thing, giving me that gift,
even adding a Grace—no mean gratuity.

11

Love customized her fingernails with his sly art,
so Heliodora's scratchies go straight to the heart.

12

You shrill-singing mosquitoes, ruthless human bloodsuckers, winged
predacious children of the night, I beg you to allow Zenophila a bit of
peaceful sleep and feed instead on me. But what's the use in asking?
Even relentless beasties like you can enjoy warming up on her tender
flesh. But I give you fair warning, nasty little things, don't make so
bold, or be prepared to meet the might of jealous hands.

13

Fly on a mission for me, mosquito,
light on the rim of Zenophila's ear,
whisper, "He lies awake and waits, while, sleepy-head,
you forget who loves you." Buzz, bizz, music-bug fly.
But speak low, don't wake up her bedmate
and make trouble for her with a jealous rival.
If you bring me the girl, mosquito, I'll hood you
with the lion's skin and put a club in your hand.

14

Love-loving Asklepias, brightly blue-eyed
as a summer sea, lures all onto her Love Boat.

15

Fair-cheeks Demo, someone makes naked merry
with your body, while inside me my heart groans.
If your lover's a Sabbath keeper, no big deal.
Love's still hot, even on chilly Sabbaths.

16

Flower-fed bee
why forsake the buds of spring
                                        and land upon
Heliodora's skin?
                    Do you mean to say
she has both sweets
                        and Love's sting,
hard to take
                and even bitter to the heart?
Yup, I think that's
                    what you're saying.
Beat it, make your philerotic beeline
back to your flowers.
                            This is old hat.

17

Dawn, love's enemy, why do you lag round the world
while another warms up beneath Demo's mantle?
But when I embraced my slender love, how quickly
you came and shed on me your Schadenfreude light.

18

I know your oath's worthless, the way your locks,
soaked with perfume, betray your wantonness.
From how your eyes, heavy with sleeplessness,
and the wreath's red ring around your head betray you.
Your curls hang loose and wild, just now mussed up,
and you're staggering around from the wine.
Get away, everybody's gal, the lyre calls you
to carousal and the clatter of castanets.

19

Have you seen this child? Love, savage Love, disappeared recently, or
possibly took off from his bed on his own. The boy can be identified
by his sweet tears and his nonstop babbling. He's swift and fearless,
laughs with a sneer, has wings on his back, over which he's slung a
quiver. Father unknown, as neither Sky, nor Earth, nor Sea will admit
to having begotten the impudent imp. He's universally hated. Love
should be considered armed and dangerous to all hearts. But wait,
there he is, near his nest! Did you think you could elude me, little
archer, by hiding in Zenophila's eyes?

20

Is it so strange
                that homicidal Love
should shoot
                fire-breathing arrows
and laugh bitterly
                with cruel looks?
After all, isn't Ares
                his mother's lover
and Hephaistos
                her lord in marriage,
the sword and forge having equal shares of her?
And his mother's mother—
                the Sea, doesn't she

howl wildly
>
> as she's whipped by the winds?

His father's nameless
>
> and lacks a pedigree.

Thus, he settles
>
> for Hephaistos' blaze,

the anger of the waves
>
> and Ares'
>>
>> blood-stained shafts.

21

I know. You didn't con me. Swearing by the gods now? I'm on to you. I get it. Stop this continuous swearing. I know all about it. That's how it was, lying girl? Alone, again? You sleep alone? Oh, the nerve! She still keeps saying it—alone! What about that stud about town, Kleon? And if not him, then—what good are threats? Just get out of my bed quick, animal! But hold it. This is exactly what you want. To see him! Oh, no, you'll stay put, my prisoner.

22

Stars, and Moon who lights the way for lovers,
and Night, and my little lyre for street party times,
shall I see this wanton one, wide awake
in her bed and crying out loud at her lamp?
Or is she with company? Then I'll hang
as petitions my tearstained garlands on her door,
inscribed thus: "Goddess, to you does Meleagros,
your initiate, offer these spoils of love."

23

If you could see Kallistion naked, stranger,
you'd suggest we switch the "th" in thighs to an "s."

24

Well, by Timo's cutely curled
love-loving ringlets

and by Demo's
sleep-depriving fragrant skin,
by that lovely Trojan foreplay
and by my wakeful lamp,
                    ever watchful
of the excitements of my carousals,
I swear to you, Love,
                    I've not much breath
left on my lips,
                which, if you want that too
just say the word
                    and I'll spit it out.

25

Timo, the hull of your racer can't hold up against the rowing of
Aphrodite's oarsmen anymore, but your upper back is bowed like a
lowered yardarm, and your gray forestays are slack, and your hanging
breasts flap like tattered sails in the wind, and your ship's belly is wrin-
kled by the splashing waves, and below she's waterlogged, flooded
with seawater, and her joints are creaky. Pity the poor bastard who,
still alive, must set sail on Lake Acheron on this gray old bag of a gal-
ley.

26

My heart's not into boy mania, Loves.
Can mounting a man be fun without give-and-take?
Love's hand in hand, and my lovely wife waits for me.
Forget about males and those holds they put on you.

27

I pray to you, Love,
                to revere my Muse,
my intercessor,
                and to put to sleep
my sleepless passion
                    for Heliodora.

I'll swear by your bow

                that's trained on me alone

and won't stop pouring

                winged shots at me.

Even if you kill me,

           I'll leave letters

to give me voice:

              "See, stranger,

                      Love's bloodied work!"

28

When Herakleitos was himself, he was a beauty.
Prime time past, his hide-bound behind blocks all mounters.
Seeing this, friend, don't be so disdainful.
Even on a rump, Nemesis can spring.

29

Thero's no longer fair in my book, and the once hot
Apollodotos's a burnt-up stick of wood.
I like loving women. Let goat-jumping herders
have their fill of these hairy-holed fairies.

30

Still a baby in his mother's lap, Love shot craps
in the morning and, wagering my soul, lost it.

31

When I see Thero, I see everything,
but everything and no Thero, nothing.

32

Praxiteles, that sculptor of old, could transform stone into a fine, if
lifeless, statue, a mute imitation of beauty. Our own Praxiteles today
practices magical animation and has molded the perfectly unscrupu-
lous Love in my heart. They are the same in name only, for his works
are better, since he doesn't transform slabs of stone but the spirit of

the mind. May he graciously shape the very type of me in such a way
as to have a temple of Love imprinted in my soul.

33

Myiskos, I'd stand up even to Zeus if I thought
he wanted to snatch you from me to pour his nectar.
Indeed, he often told me himself, "Why worry?
Nothing to be jealous about. I've learned compassion."
So he says, but should I even hear a fly buzz,
I'd fear that all his talk had proved to be a lie.

34

Self-deceiving
lovesick boy-love
bitter honey-
lipped burn victims,
pour cold water
ice-cold water
over my heart.
For I have seen
D i o n y s o s.
My fellow slaves,
don't let this fire
run to my guts.

35

I tried to run from Love, but he lit up
a torch from the ashes and found me hiding.
Didn't bend his bow, but between his fingertips
pinched a bit of fire and, unseen, flicked it at me.
Now I'm engulfed by flames. O Phanion,
you little spark, you've set my heart ablaze.

36

"The die is cast. Light the torch. I'm on my way."
"Well, looky here. Such daring. And all wined up!"

"You should care? I'm taking the party to her. Hear!"
"Where are you off to, my good mind?"
"Does love have to give reasons? Light up. Now!"
"What about your old studies in logic?"
"Good-bye to study hall wisdom. I know one thing:
Love cleaned out even the above-it-all mind of Zeus."

37

Didn't I cry out to you, my soul?
Didn't I give warning?
                    "O my lovesick,
you'll be taken,
                    sure as Aphrodite rules,
for you'll keep flying
                    right into her trap."
                                        Well, didn't I?
And you're caught.
                    So why fight it?
Love himself has tied your wings
and set you on the fire
                    and sprinkles your face
with fragrance
                    when you faint,
and when you thirst
                    gives you hot tears to drink.

38

In a summertime thirst, I kissed a tender boy,
and said, after I'd satisfied that parching thirst,
"Is this not Ganymede's libation to your lips,
Father Zeus, when you drink up his kiss of nectar?"
For now that I've kissed our most beautiful young man,
Antiochos, I've tasted the soul's sweet honey.

39

Kidnapped!
                Who would do such violence?
Who'd start a war with Love himself?
The torches, quick!
                Wait, footsteps?
                        Heliodora!
Hop back home into my breast,
                heart!

40

The skipper's Aphrodite,
                Love mans the tiller,
handling the end of my soul's rudder,
and passion's heavy gale tosses me up
into a sea of boys
                of every stripe
as I swim off the coast
                of Fire Island.

41

How sweet it is to mix wine with the bee's liquor,
and sweet to love a boy when one is lovely, too,
the way Alex is in love with soft-haired Kleon.
Such a couple's a blend of Kypris' deathless mead.

42

Aphrodite sets the fires for women,
but her boy, Love, takes good care of the men.
So where do I go? With Mom? Or the brat?
I'll bet even she admits, "The pushy kid wins."

NOSSIS

(early third century B.C.)

Nothing is sweeter than love, all of life's blessings
come in second. I have even spat out honey.
I, Nossis, say this, but one Kypris has not kissed
will not ever know what roses her flowers are.

> (*or*)

Is anything sweeter than love?
                    None of life's blessings
can beat it.
         I'll even spit honey out of my mouth.
I, Nossis, say this,
         but someone Kypris has never kissed
cannot begin to know
         the flowering of the rose.

PLATO

(ca. 427–347 B.C.)

1

Nine muses, you say? Look again:
Sappho the Lesbian makes it ten!

2

When I kissed Agathon, my soul rose to my lips,
in hopes, poor thing, of making the great leap across.

3

I'm the apple pitched at you by a would-be lover.
Nod yes, Xanthippe—you and I, we're on the wane.

4

To Aphrodite, I, whose proud beauty
made a mockery of Greece, I, Laïs,
who had young lovers flocking to my door,
offer my mirror, since I cannot bear
the sight of me as I am,

                    the loss of me as I was.

POSEIDIPPOS

(fl. 280 B.C.)

1

Shower us, Attic jug, let Bacchus wet us down.
Yes, shower us and refresh our drinking party.
Quiet, Zeno, learned swan, and Kleanthes' Muse,
the only singing here's of sweet-then-bitter Love.

2

You can't fool me, Philainis, with crocodile tears.
I know, you love me more than anybody else—
as long as you are lying beside me.
But beside someone else—you'd tell the same story.

3

Sure, sure, shoot me, Loves.
I'll be your target.
Spare me not, silly boys.
If you defeat me
you'll become famous
among immortals
as first-rate archers
and as the masters
of a mighty quiver.

4

Well-armed, I'll fight you and not give up, Love,
though I'm only human. So back away.
If you come upon me drunk, take me prisoner,
but as long as I'm sober, Reason stands by me.

5

Goddess, who haunts Kypros and Kythera,
Miletos, and Syria's hoofbeat-thundered fair plain,
come, please come kindly to Kallistion, who
never shut her door in a lover's face.

6

If Pythias has someone with her, so long;
if in bed alone, let me in for a bit, by God.
Then say that drunk I passed thieves to come,
possessed by bold Love as my guide.

7

Tears and parties, why do you drop me before my feet
can cool off onto another of Kypris' beds of hot coals?
I'll never stop loving and my lack of discernment
keeps bringing me new hurt from Aphrodite.

RHIANOS

(ca. 200 B.C.)

O lovely butt,
                  sweetly oiled up
by the Hours and Graces
                        you won't let even old men sleep.
Tell me,
             whose piece of bliss you are
and which of the boys
                you adorn.
And it answered,
                "I belong to Daddy—Menekrates."

FROM

The Garland of Philippos of Thessalonika

ANTIPHILOS

(first century A.D.)

Here's the Laconian river Eurotas,
Leda with nothing on, Zeus hidden in the swan.
Loves, why do you test me so? Me a bird?
If Zeus is a swan, then I'm a white duck.

AUTOMEDON

(no date)

1

Yesterday I dined with Demetrios, that most blessed of all men, the
Boys' Coach. One was sprawled on his lap, one hung over his shoulder,
and two others served his food and drink—what a terrific little team. I
couldn't help wisecracking, "Good buddy, do you work out the boys at
night, too?"

2

The dancing girl from Asia, who strikes up
lewd poses, vibrating down to her fingertips,
I praise, yet not that she shows all passions,
or waves her supple arms softly here and there,
but that she can flit around a worn-down peg
and not be turned off by old age's wrinkles.
She gives it tongue, she gives it fun, a firm grip,
and, kicking up her legs, a brand-new life.

BASSUS

(early first century A.D.)

Turn into gold?
        A bull?
            A swan?
Me?
    I don't think so.
        I can't fly.
I leave such games to Zeus,
        and pay the girl her price.

DIODOROS

(first century B.C.)

Listen, son of my important friend, take my advice
and even though he makes your eyes water with desire
for that god-given body of his, stop twirling
around that pretty boy. Neither kind nor guileless,
he's no greenhorn at love, and many pursue him.
His company's way too fast for you, young fellow.

KRINAGORAS

(first century B.C.)

Krinagoras, unless the lovely Gemella
lie at your side, sleepless your rest must be,
and no rest at all, tossing and turning
back and forth all over your empty bed.

MACCIUS

(early first century B.C.?)

I swore by your name, Love's Goddess, to avoid
Hedylion for two nights. I think you smiled,
knowing what I was going through. But I won't
keep the second, casting my oath to the winds.
I'd prefer to sin against you for her sake
than keep my word and die of piety.

MARCUS ARGENTARIUS

(fl. turn of the first century B.C./A.D.)

1

Everything the flower-loving bee you're named for does,
you do, my Melissa, and I take it to heart.
You drop honey from your lips when you sweetly kiss,
and when you want money, can give a mean sting.

2

To follow your discerning eye
and fall for a beauty's not love.
But looking at someone homely,
heart inflamed, you bite the arrow—
now that's love, that's fire. The beauties
please everyone with a good eye.

3

A skinny
Aphrodite
Dioclea
but so sweet.
There's not much
between us
so falling
on her flat
chest I lie
on her heart.

4

Lysidike, tease, take off that netting,
and don't sway your hips so as you approach.
Your flimsy, see-through dress clings well to you,
makes you seem naked without being so.
If you think it would be fun, I too will dress
in something gauzy and hide my hard-on.

5

For my toast to Lysidike pour me
ten measures, to longed-for Euphrante's one.
Think I love Lysidike more?— Oh, no,
by sweet Bacchus, to whom I drain this cup.
Euphrante's one equals ten. Like the moon,
doesn't its light outshine the countless stars?

6

When you were rich, my friend, you fell in love.
Now poor, no love. A fine cure is hunger.
Menophila, who once called you "sweetie"
and "handsome Adonis," now asks your name.
"Who? From where?" You've caught on to the saying
"Nobody loves you when you're down and out."

7

Loving women is best for certain kinds of men,
those who take relationships seriously.
But if you're also into loving males,
I can teach you the cure for that mad lovesickness.
Just flip the lovely-thighed Menophila,
and pretend you have Menophilos below.

8

I had a big thing for young Alkippe,
and succeeding in getting her to bed,

our hearts were pounding in case some third wheel
surprised us in the act of secret love.
But her mother overheard her chatter,
and averred, "Share and share alike, my girl."

9

You think your sucking off young men is a secret,
Heraklea. But no, it's the talk of the town.
Now how could you behave so badly? Did someone
grab you by those gorgeous locks and force you down?
Or is it because you're named after Herakles,
dirty girl, and think that kissing cock's heroic?

PHILODEMOS

(ca. 110–30 B.C.)

1

Douse the lamp with oil, Philainis,
that mute watcher of private affairs,
then exit yourself (Love wants no one looking),
and shut the door tight. Now in you come
Xantho, my friend. And you, hot bed of passions,
take these lessons we press on you.

2

Sixty times has Grace gone round with the sun
but the dark sheen of her hair has not gone,
and so too the marble cones of her breasts
stand firm and free of any foundation.
Her flawless body glistens heavenly,
she fascinates and lives up to her name.
So step up you red-hot well-hung lovers
and lose track of her threescore years.

3

Hel-lo!
    Hi!
What's your name?
        What's yours?
Don't come on so.
        Ditto.
Got a date?
        With whoever wants me.

How about dinner?
>If you say so.
Okay, what'll it cost?
>Nothing down.
Funny girl.
>Play me, then pay me.
Alright, where can I send for you?
>>Take it down.
And you'll come?
>Anytime.
Like now?
>Let's go.

4

Whenever I hold Kydilla tight, come I
by day or with a lot of nerve by night,
I know I walk the line right on the edge,
lay my life on a high roll of the dice.
What good's it to me? Reckless Love, when you
have me in tow, I don't see fear's shadow.

5

Demo and Thermion both slay me—
one's a pro, the other still unversed in your ways,
the one I can grope, the other mustn't touch.
I swear, Goddess, I don't know which I want more.
I'll say little virgin Demo—I don't want it off the rack,
but long for what's under lock and key.

6

"Darling, I know how to return love
and how to give back bite for bite.
Don't overvex your lover or
ignite a poet's deepest anger."
I kept warning you, but you paid

about as much attention as Lake Michigan.
Now tears run down your tits
and I lay my head in Flo's.

7

I loved—who hasn't? I worshipped—hasn't
everyone been in that congregation?
But I was crazy—did a god do it?
The force that through my black hair drives the gray
announces the age of reason—I'm done.
At playtime I played, now I'll act my age.

8

I fell in love with Demo from Paphos—
no wonder. Then with Demo from Samos—
not such a big deal. Then with Demo
auf Naxos—now it's no longer child's play:
Demo number four is from Argos. Seems
the Fates have named me eponymously
for my pandemic affections ...

9

Round midnight through the rain
out of my husband's bed
soaked to the skin I came.
So we sit doing zero
not gurgling and dozing
like lovers are supposed to?

10

Philainion's petite and on the dark side,
kinkier than parsley, softer than down,
a voice more magic than divine lingerie,
and does everything yet asks for nothing
usually. O, I'll take her, golden Kypris,
till I uncover one that's better.

11

Shine on, horny Moon, for all-night stands
shine right through the window screen—
spotlight priceless Kallistion. Deathless,
you peer without spite on lover's bedwork.
I know we have your blessing, Moon—
didn't Endymion light up your soul?

12

Your summer bud's not yet blown
nor that charming bunch of virgin grapes full ripe
and already the young Loves file their darts,
Lysidike, and a fire smolders out of sight.
Let's run, so lovesick, before the arrow's strung.
I feel a blaze coming on.

13

Whoosis pays What's-her-face a pile for just once
and suffers goose bumps screwing an unattractive girl.
I pay Lysianassa a few bucks for a dozen
and screw the clearly better-looking woman.
Well, either I'm out of my mind or he ought to lay
his twin whatchamacallits on the chopping block!

14

For style on the lyre, voice, meaningful eyes, and song
it's Xanthippe, and this brand-new fire will burn you,
my heart—exactly how or when I'm not sure,
but you'll know it, poor thing, when you've caught on.

15

O feet, shins, thighs that just destroy me,
O buns, bush, and flanks,
shoulders, breasts, O slender tender neck,
arms, eyes that drive me crazy,

O movement most artful, soul kisses
supreme, O little cries that stir me!
So what if Flora's Italian and can't sing Sappho,
Perseus loved Andromeda the Indian.

16

You cry, whine, peer strangely at me,
you're jealous, cling and clutch, kiss too much:
now that's a lover. But when you say, "Here I Am,"
and just lay back, you make me wonder.

17

Xantho, girl of wax, with scented skin and Muse's face,
sweet-voiced, beautiful gift of the twin-winged Loves,
play for me with your fragrant, shining hands:
"On a single-bed cut of stone I must sleep,
though I must live a long, long time." Please, again,
yes, dear, yes, with that same sweet song.

18

I who was once good, Aphrodite, for five to nine
now barely manage the first between sundown and up
(mostly down). Good grief, this thing (that's often suffered
half-deaths) is just dying! And the only perfect fit
is the punishment to the crime. Old age, what will you do
once you come if I'm this droopy now?

19

Of violets white and lively lyres,
of Chian wine and Syrian myrrh,
of cutting up and thirsty whores,
I've had my fill: foolish things I hate.
Now tie narcissus in my hair, and toot
the crooked flute, rub my limbs with saffron oil,
wet my whistle with wine of Mytilene,
and pair me with a virgin who loves her nest.

20

Thirty-seven years have already turned,
pages torn out of my life's work;
already my hair's sprouting whites,
messengers, Xanthippe, of wisdom's age.
But the lyricism of carousal—I
still care for, and a hungry fire burns in my heart.
So write me an ending with a flourish, Muses,
to my madness with this very girl.

FROM
THE CYCLE OF
AGATHIAS SCHOLASTIKOS

1

I'm not into wine
but you can get me drunk
                                    if you taste first
and then I'll take it
                        when offered.
Once your lips touch it,
it's impossible to abstain
                                    or refuse the sweet giver
for the cup ferries your kiss to me
                                            and proclaims
its joy in what it tasted first.

2

May Aphrodite herself and her charming Loves
waste my empty heart for contempt of me
if I ever start loving men. May I never
succeed or slide into that graver sin.
Bad enough to offend with women, which I'll do,
but leave the young men to that fool, Pittalakos.

3

To Paulos Silentiarius from the opposite side of the Bosporus:
This place, completely dressed in green, attains the full beauty of
its rich flora, and, in the shade of cypress trees, birds, already mothers
of tender chicks, are warbling. The goldfinch sings its shrill little
song and the mourning dove moans from its thorny thicket. What

pleasure can I take in this, I, who would rather hear your voice than the strains of Apollo's harp? Two loves beset me. I yearn to see you, my good friend, and to see my sweetie-pie, the thought of whom consumes me. But my study of the Law keeps me away from my lovely lady.

LEONTIOS

(sixth century A.D.)

Touch, cup, those honeydew lips. Press your luck.
I don't envy you. I just should be so lucky.

MAKEDONIOS HYPATOS

(fl. A.D. 500)

1

"See you tomorrow." Which never comes,
what with your way of piling up your put-offs.
I want you and that's what you give me; for others
you have presents, but for me broken promises.
"See you this evening." But what's evening for women?
Old age with wrinkles, countless wrinkles.

2

Please, Love, stop hitting me in the heart and liver.
If shoot you must, try for some other part.

3

Grace blooms from your mouth, flowers from your cheeks,
Love from your eyes, and music from your hands.
You capture eyes with flashing eyelids, ears with song.
With every part you put young men in misery.

4

I go after Love with gold.
                              After all, bees work
with spring's fresh flowers,
                              not spade or plow.
And gold turns out to be
                              the specialist
for getting Aphrodite's honey.

5

In a dream, I grabbed hold of this laughter-loving girl. She gave in to
me completely and did not object to a single thing I did or asked for.
But Love, full of jealousy, ambushed me even at night, and, cutting off
my sleep, tipped over and spilled my cup of bliss. So invidious Love
allows me no satisfaction, not even in my dreams.

6

Constance, but not in deed. Still, I thought you might be
so, indeed, when I heard you say your pretty name.
But you're worse than death. Dump him who loves you,
chase him who doesn't, and then dump him when he does.
Your mouth's a hook, Connie, tipped with madness.
I bit, and now just hang there from your red, red lips.

PALLADAS

(fourth century A.D.)

I charge Zeus with not being much of a lover,
since he didn't shift shape for this proud beauty's sake.
For in looks she holds her own against Europa,
against Danae, or even tender Leda.
I guess he doesn't care for whores, for I know
the only goods he wants are royal virgins.

PAULOS SILENTIARIUS

(fl. A.D. 563)

1

Reply to his friend Agathias:
Love is a battler and knows nothing about Law, nor should any other occupation tear a man away from his mad passion. If your dedication to your law studies holds you back, then there's no fierce love beating under your breast. What kind of love is it that lets a narrow strait of water keep you from your beloved? Leandros showed the power of his love by his fearless swimming through the billows and the night. And remember, my friend, you need only take the ferry. No, you have renounced Aphrodite and have committed to Athena. To the latter belongs the law, to the former, desire. You tell me, who's the man that can serve them both at once?

2

Let's drop our clothes, babe, and press skin
on skin, your legs with mine entwine.
Nothing between us. Even that flimsy
thing seems like the wall Semiramis built
in Babylon. Let's connect at the breast
and lips. Then silence. I really hate babble.

3

As a golden ray
               penetrating Danae's
               bronze chamber
Zeus slipped the knot
                   of her virginity *intacta.*

What does this story mean?
Here's what I think:
"Gold rules
over brazen walls and chains.
Gold unties all tethers
and opens every lock.
Gold brings those raised eyebrows
to their knees.
It was what undid
the will of Danae."
So lover,
why pray to Aphrodite
when you've got
cold cash in hand.

4

Rhodope, let's steal our kisses and the lovely
hard-earned labors of Kyprian Aphrodite.
How sweet it is to elude nosy surveillance.
Love affairs should be tightly sealed in honey jars.

5

Doris pulled out
one of her golden hairs
and bound my hands,
taking me prisoner.
First, I laughed,
thinking it would be easy
to shake off
the attractive Doris' fetters,
but I soon discovered
I hadn't the strength
and began to groan
like someone shackled
in irons.

Now, no more Mr. Lucky,
> I'm hung on a hair
and must go anywhere
> my headmistress drags me.

6

Kissing Hippomenes, my heart shifts to Leandros, and while fastened on to Leandros' lips, I fantasize about Xanthos, and, while I'm wrapped all around Xanthos, my heart returns to Hippomenes. So I keep dropping him I have in hand, taking on one after the other over and over in my arms, paying court to Love's riches. He who blames me can go straight to the poorhouse of monogamy.

7

Sure, maybe the hellish pain Tantalos endures
is lighter than mine.
> He never laid eyes on you,
was never denied the touch of your lips,
softer than a rose cup.
> Tantalos,
weeping nonstop, cringes under the rock overhead,
but he can't die again,
> and I'm still alive,
>> barely,
wasting away by desire
> to the very edge.

8

Sappho's soft all over, and soft are her kisses,
and soft's the state of her snow-white embrace.
But her hard heart's made of stone. And her love
terminates at her lips—below the neck, nada.
Maybe he who can take this, maybe he
can easily take on Tantalos' thirst.

9

The bite of a mad dog, they say, makes a man see
the hydrophobic brute's image in the water.
I wonder if Love turned rabid before he sank
his cruel fangs into me and made my heart go mad.
For now your lovely face keeps looking back at me
in the sea, the swirling river, and my wine cup.

RUFINUS DOMESTICUS

(probably sixth century A.D.)

I like everything about you except
your undiscerning eye for low-life men.

OTHER POETS IN
THE GREEK ANTHOLOGY

ARCHIAS

(first century B.C.?)

1

Your advice I "avoid Love" makes for lost labor.
On foot, I should outrun such diving, winged pursuit?

2

Take up your bow, Goddess, and shoot at someone else.
No room on my poor body for another arrow.

CAPITO

(no date)

Beauty without grace can only please, not secure
—like floating bait without a hook.

DIONYSIOS SOPHISTES

(second century A.D.?)

You with the roses, you're pretty rosy yourself.
So what's for sale? You? The roses? Or both?

DIOPHANES OF MYRINA

(no date)

There are three good reasons for calling Love a crook:
he's always on the take, he's reckless, he cleans up.

GALLUS

(no date)

Lydie, who can take on three men at a time,
one on top, one below, and one behind,
says, "Welcome, buggers, fuckers, and kinkies.
In a hurry? You and two friends? Well, step right up!"

KILLAKTOR

(no date)

A young girl fills her piggy bank,
not through her skill but her stuff.

NIKARCHOS

(first century A.D.)

A fine, bigly built woman I fancy,
Sam, in her prime time or over the hill.
If young one can wrap her big legs round me,
then wrinkle-faced old one can blow me.

NOUMENIOS OF TARSOS

(no date)

Ross is Boss. I should care he's less than a letter off?
I'm not supposed to read the hunk, just gaze at him.

RUFINUS

(date uncertain)

1

Much joy from Rufinus to his sweetie, Elpis,
if joy apart from me were possible.
I swear by your eyes I can no longer abide
this desolate, lonely bed without you.
Well, awash in tears I'll visit Koressos hill
or the temple of Artemis the Great.
But tomorrow I'm back in our hometown, and I'll
fly into view with a thousand blessings.

2

Prodike, let's bathe, wear crowns, unwatered
wine down, raising the biggest cups around.
Brief is rejoicing's life, and then old age
cuts down what's left, and at the end comes death.

3

Europa's kiss may taste sweet upon your lips,
light upon your mouth, but her own open lips
and tight-fitting mouth can suck the soul
all the way up from your fingertips.

4

So where's Praxiteles and good-hands Polykleitos,
who put soul into ancient works of art?
Who will fashion Melite's fragrant curls,
her burning eyes and lustrous neck?

Where are the shapers, the sculptors? Such beauty,
like a god's image, demands its temple.

5

Hailed no more as mad about boys, but now into
women, I've switched from boys' toys to the girls'.
No more boys with pure complexions for me,
but faces made up with powders and rouge.
Dolphins will graze in mountain forests,
fleet-footed deer on the foamy, white sea.

6

Rhodope, Melite, and Rhodokleia contested
which of them was best between the thighs,
and asked me to referee; like divine beauty queens,
they stood there naked, drenched with nectar.
Between Rhodope's thighs shined the Cyclops' eye
like a thick rosebush cleft by a western breeze.
[*two lines missing*]
Rhodokleia's was smooth as glass, a moistened front,
like a temple statue that's just been sculpted.
But wise to what Paris suffered for his decision,
I declared a three-way tie, awarding the prize to all.

7

To you, Boopie, sweet-giver Love me gave as slave,
a compliant bull, subjugated by desire,
and all too willing, completely at your service,
never to seek his bitter liberation
till he grow old and gray, dear. Let no evil eye
ever blight or put a hex upon our hopes.

8

So now, Melissa, what's happened to your
golden, talk-of-the-town, famous beauty?
Where those eyebrows, disdainful looks, long neck,

and your rich, gold jangling ankle bracelets?
Now your horrid hair's unwashed, feet in rags.
That's what happens to brazen, heedless whores.

9

I judged three bottoms, whose owners chose me,
showing off their bared splendid lower halves.
The first had smiling dimples pressed in hers,
glittering white cheeks, so soft to the touch.
The second's pair were snowy white and blushed
a deeper red than the most crimson rose.
The third's a calm sea furrowed by a silent wave,
her luscious flesh rippling naturally.
If Paris had seen three asses like these,
he'd fully forget those divine behinds of old.

10

Who battered and tossed you out half-naked?
Who has stones for eyes, and for a heart, too?
Maybe he came too soon, caught you with a lover.
It happens. You all do it, pussycat.
Next time, when someone's in and he is out,
lock the front door, lest it happen again.

11

Don't like them easy, don't like them shy.
One gives it too fast, the other too slow.

12

Sunfish and Skiff, a couple of sleek whores,
are always riding just off the harbor.
Run for your lives, boys, from Aphrodite's pirates.
He who screws around with them, goes under.

13

Thalia, I've often prayed for one night with you,
to fulfill my desire for mad love's bounty.
Now that I have your sweet naked body next to me,
I'm spent, all tuckered out and drowsy.
Miserable desire, what's happened to you?
You should be so lucky another day.

14

Lucky me to see Prodike alone, I pitched,
and hugging her ambrosial knees, I said,
"Save a man wasting away bit by bit,
and grant me what little breath I have left."
She wept to hear me say this, wiped her tears,
and with her dainty hands, pushed me away.

15

Aphrodite, I'd this young neighbor girl,
Amy, who set a big fire in my heart.
The kid joked around with me, and I seized the day.
She'd blush. A bigger turn-on. She felt the itch, too.
My pains paid off. Now I hear she's knocked up.
So what do I do? Split or stick around?

16

If women were as charming after as before,
men would never tire of fucking their wives,
but after, they're all back to unpleasant.

17

Melissa denies she's in love, but her body,
a quiverful of arrows, screams another story.
Her step's unsteady, her breathing unstable,
and under her eyes hang deep, dark hollows.

You Loves, do this for your fair-wreathed Mother,
burn this rebel till she cry, "I'm on fire!"

18

Fireman Love, if you can't torch two together,
put out the flame that burns up one or transfer it.

19

Rhodope basks in her beauty. If I say, "Hi,"
she'll only reply by raising her eyebrows.
If I ever hang flowers on her door,
she'll stomp them with her angry little heels.
Wrinkles and brutal old age, come prematurely,
please hurry. You at least can bring down Rhodope.

20

For how long, Prodike, should I weep at your door?
How long, Stonewall, will you be deaf to my prayers?
Already gray hairs begin to besiege you.
Soon we'll look like Hecuba and Priam making it.

SKYTHINOS

(early second century A.D.?)

1

I'm beset by a great woe, a great war, a great fire. Elissos is ripe for love, a deadly sixteen, possessed of every charm, great and small, a reading voice and kissing lips of honey, and a thing most perfect for taking in. What can I do? He allows me looking only. I'll just have to keep on lying awake, engaged in hand-to-hand combat with this empty love.

2

Mr. No-name, now you're erect, won't wilt at all,
and into stretching like there's no tomorrow.
But when Nemesenos surrendered and bent himself
to me, you just hung there like a dead man. So go stretch,
burst apart, shed your tears, all for nothing.
And don't expect compassion from this hand.

STRATON

(fl. A.D. 125)

1

The appendages of boys, Diodoros, fall
into three phases, and you should learn to name them:
call the one that's mature but still untouched "lalou,"
"koko" call the one that's just beginning to bulge;
to the one now surging upon your hand, say "lizard,"
but for one more perfect, you'll know the swellest name.

2

I like a pale face fine,
                              also skin the color of honey,
and a fair-haired boy, too.
                              Then again, black hair
can get me going,
                              and I can't overlook big brown eyes,
yet must admit
                  flashing black eyes
                                          are over the top.

3

The letters in *proktos* and *chrysos* have the same
numerical value, which I found out by chance.

      (*or*)

Anus and *gold* in Greek add up to the same sum:
one, five, seven, oh, what an accident!

4

Now with a young girl
                   we're not talking
genuine sphincter,
              a simple kiss,
                             natural-smelling skin,
nor of that endearing dirty talk
                   or limpid look.
The more you teach her
              the worse she is.
Besides, they're all cold
            back there.
                 And the bigger problem—
there's no place
        to affix
              your roaming hand.

5

Earlier in the day, he happened to pass
the store where they make garlands and saw a boy
weaving flowers with berries, and found himself moved.
He approached and asked about their quality,
and then, somewhat more quietly, for how much
would the boy sell him his garland. The boy blushed
redder than his roses and, bending his head,
told him to leave fast, lest his father see him.
As a pretense he bought a wreath and went home,
crowned his gods, and begged them to answer his prayer.

6

You've become a beauty, Diodoros, and ripe for lovers.
But go right ahead and get married, we won't abandon you.

7

Yesterday I had
                Philostratos for the night
and couldn't do a thing,
                   though—
how can I put it?
              —he was accommodating
in every way.
              Throw me off a tower,
like baby Astyanax,
                friends,
since I'm no longer
              one of your stand-up guys.

8

Long hair and superfluous ringlets charm me not,
for they're taught in the school of Art, not of Nature,
but the dusty grime of a boy in the palaestra
and the sheen of limbs rubbed down in oil, do.
I'll take my sweet passion without embellishment.
Bewitching beauty's female Aphrodite's work.

9

Why so gloomy, Menippos, draped to your ankles,
you who once so proudly displayed most of your leg?
Why do you pass in silence and with downcast eyes?
I know, you're hiding those things I told you would come.

10

Those hoity-toity boys
                with their purple-edged robes,
that you and I
             haven't a prayer of getting at,

Diphilos,
        are like ripe figs
                  up on rocky ridges
that the vultures and ravens
              feast upon.

11

While bathing yesterday,
             Diokles
raised up a lizard
          from the tub,
a veritable *Aphrodite Rising.*
                  If Paris, up in Ida,
had seen it,
          he would have called off
the big three-goddess contest.

12

Count all on the bed a threesome,
but with two actives, two passives.
Looks like a miracle? No lie.
Middleman does two-way service.

13

The neighbor's small, tender boy really turns me on,
and his laugh signs experience and willingness.
He's but twelve, and the unripe grapes are unguarded.
When he matures, both stakes and watchmen will be set.

14

If you were quite inexperienced in the thing about which I'm trying to persuade you, you'd be right to be afraid, thinking it could be something awful. But if your master's bed has made you expert in it, why begrudge the gift of receiving it to another? For he, being your lord, after having you sent in to do his bidding, dismisses you without a word and goes to sleep. But here you'll have other pleasures, like playing as an equal and chatting with each other, and anything else, an invitation, not an order.

15

Now you're up, damn thing, good wood with nothing there.
Yesterday there was, you couldn't heave one breath of air.

16

Once, when given the opportunity, a wrestling coach, while training a smooth-skinned boy, took him down to his knees and started to put a bear hug around his waist from behind with one arm, while feeling up the berries with the other. But as chance would have it, the master of the house came in and asked for the boy. The coach quickly flipped him on his back and put a choke hold on him. But the master of the house, who knew a thing or two about wrestling, said to him, "Better stop whatever tight fit you're trying to put to the boy."

17

Agathon's lizard was rosy-fingered
just the other day, now it's rosy-armed.

18

I know a eunuch served by lovely boys.
To what end? For he harms them against nature's laws.
Really, like the dog in the manger with roses,
he howls, and does himself no good, nor them.

19

You lean your lovely cheeks against the wall, Cy.
Why? Why do you tempt stone, which can do nothing?

20

And so now my temples have turned all gray,
and my dick hangs between my thighs, useless.
My balls don't work, and unbearable old age comes.
Oh, boy! My buggery's confined to the mind.

21

Can it ever seem to one
his beloved's past his prime,
if they're always together,
if they are never apart?
Can he who pleased yesterday
fail to please again today?
And if he is pleasing now,
how displeasing tomorrow?

ANONYMOUS POEMS

1

That high-end whore who's set this town on fire,
whose breath of gold attracts all who want her,
lay by me naked all night in a dream,
giving herself to me gratis until sweet dawn.
Now I needn't beg this stranger, nor feel
sorry for myself, since Sleep does the trick.

2

Two woes have I. I'm poor and I'm in love.
First's easy, second's too hot to handle.

3

Fell in love, kissed, got lucky, and was loved.
But the who and how, Goddess only knows.

4

Eagle-Zeus came to godlike Ganymede,
as a swan to Helen's fair-haired mother.
There's no comparison between the two,
some like one, some the other. Me, both.

5

I'd love to be the seaside breeze
that blows on you walking topless.

6

Oh, to be that pink rose you plucked
and set between your snow-white breasts.

7

I send you perfume, not to honor you
but it in the wearing. You're the perfume.

8

Girl playing lyre, I'd like to step up and pluck
your top string, and then pull the one called G.

9

Hello, young lady.
                        Hello.
Who's that in front of you?
                                  What's it to you?
Oh, I have my reasons.
                           My mistress.
Do I have a chance?
                      For what?
One night.
               What's in it for her?
Gold coin.
               There's hope.
This much.
               Forget about it.

10

Niko's love charm
carved of clear amethyst
set in gold
and hung on a thread
of purple wool
that can haul
a man across the sea
or a boy
out of his room
to you to keep

Aphrodite she
the witch of Larissa
gives.

11

When a green grape,
                      you said, "No!"
When ripe,
           "Get lost!"
Now may I nibble
                on your raisin?

12

Women's love leaves my heart cold, but not men's,
whose torches smother me with coals of fire.
Just as a man's stronger than a woman,
so much hotter and keener's this passion.

13

Be friends?
                Would like to, but can't.
You won't ask for
                    or accept what I can give
nor give
            what I would ask of you.

14

Don't pull my cloak off, mister, but look at me
as a figure draped in wood with marble limbs.
If it's the naked grace of Antiphilos
you want, you'll find that rose growing among thorns.

15

Look, Aribazos, you can't burn up all Knidos.
Its very stone is crumbling in the heat.

16

You're beautiful, Persian mothers, you and your babies,
but beautiful Aribazos surpasses beauty.

17

I don't see the lovely Dionysos around.
Did you pick him up—Big Daddy Zeus—
to be second cupbearer of the gods?
Hey, eagle—when your feathered glory
caught up that pretty boy, did he take on
scratch marks from your claws before you let him drop?

18

King Zeus, enjoy your old boy Ganymede,
and gaze at my Dexandros from afar.
I've no grudge. But if you take my fair boy by force,
I shan't endure your tyranny nor life itself.

19

I ask you, Graces, if I be Dionysos' choice,
extend his beauty through the seasons forever.
If he, passing on me, settles on another,
sweep him out like dust and a stale myrtle berry.

20

When Menecharmos won the boxing match,
I crowned him with ten soft ribbons,
and gave his bloodied-up face three kisses,
but sweeter than myrrh it tasted to me.

21

Why so noisy, chattering birds? Don't vex me,
when I'm in heaven next to this boy's soft body.
Sleep, you nightingales perching in the leaves,
I beg you, loquacious females. Shut up!

22

If among the boys, stranger,

        you saw one whose bloom
was most lovely,

    then it was Apollodotos you saw,
and having seen him,

      if you weren't overpowered
by blazing desire,

    you must be a god

        or a stone.

NOTES TO THE

TRANSLATOR'S PREFACE

1. This account, being tailored to a reader's edition of translations, is intended as a concise explanation of an extremely complex literary and scholarly matter that has raised many questions, only a fraction of which have been satisfactorily answered. Those interested in doing further reading in this area should consult the magisterial work of Alan Cameron, *The Greek Anthology, from Meleager to Planudes* (Oxford: Clarendon Press, 1993), and Kathryn J. Gutzwiller's richly informative study *Poetic Garlands: Hellenistic Epigrams in Context* (Berkeley: University of California Press, 1998). For a selective but fairly extensive overview in English of all of the great anthology's contents, see Peter Jay, editor, *The Greek Anthology and Other Ancient Epigrams* (New York: Penguin Books, 1981). See the entries under Rufinus and Straton in the Notes section below for more detailed explanations of their representation in *The Palatine Anthology*.

2. Greek and Latin verse is quantitative, that is, based on metrical patterns of long and short vowels rather than on sequences of stressed and unstressed syllables, as in our own system of versification. Ancient Greek prosody, however, also involved accent and pitch and is generally considered to have been among the most complex in world literature. In these translations, I have chosen to focus primarily upon what I can do for the sound of the poem in American English rather than to attempt metrical approximations of poems we can never truly hear in their actual, original articulation.

3. Eliot Weinberger, trans., "The Homeric Versions," in *Selected Fictions*, ed. Weinberger (New York: Penguin Books, 1999), p. 69.

Notes

ANAKREON of Teos, a Greek city in western Asia Minor, was one of Greece's most famous poets. Named as one of the nine poets in the Alexandrian canon (see *The Greek Anthology,* Book 9.184), he wrote poems, largely but not exclusively in celebration of the pleasures of life, that were widely imitated. According to legend, he choked to death on a grape seed. Meleagros included a handful of Anakreon's poems in his anthology, but none of these are amatory epigrams.

1

I have taken the liberty of inserting the epithet "Lord Loud-Shout" in the first line from a small fragment of Anakreon's in which Dionysos is described as "often loud-shouting." My capitalization of the god's name a few lines later is another modification for the sake of emphasis. Also called Bacchus, Dionysos was the god of the vine, of wine and religious ecstasy.

The name Eros, for the god of love and the son of Aphrodite, has been translated as "Love" throughout this book. While this god has a complex history, his identity in these poems remains the familiar one of the winged god of love who primarily instigates crushes and passionate attachments for specific individuals. His more famous mother, Aphrodite, generally represents the universal sexual principle of the cosmos, which Greek myth and literature depict as holding sway over mortals and immortals alike. Poets and lovers revere, appeal to, and complain to both mother and son habitually. According to one tradition, Aphrodite bore two sons, to whom some of our poets refer as "the Loves" or "twin Loves."

11

Some ancient authorities thought this poem was addressed to Sappho. By translating the Greek pronoun for "another," which would denote either a "man" or a "woman" according to the masculine and feminine gender forms in which it is given in different textual readings of this poem, as "someone else" I have sought to preserve the ambiguity of its history rather than to force a choice.

ARCHILOCHOS was the bastard son of an aristocrat of the Cycladic island of Paros and a slave woman. A mercenary soldier and a poet of great originality, he died in battle and was revered by the Greeks for generations for his innovations in versification, language, and content, which was strongly personal. Almost all of his surviving work is fragmentary.

1

Like several others before me, I have fused these two closely related fragments into a single but still fragmentary poem by inserting a lacuna between them.

3

The epithet "limb-loosener" (*lusimeles*), which Archilochos uses here in apposition to "desire" (*pothos*), was commonly used, as in Sappho's Poem 4, to describe the power of Love to make a man or woman go weak in the knees over another.

4

Some scholars question the attribution of this poem to Archilochos. The word "fig" was often used as a metaphor for vagina, and the poet uses it elsewhere.

6

In Cologne, in 1973, this fragment was discovered on a scrap of mummy wrapping. It was edited and published by R. Merkelbach and M. West in 1974 and was an immediate sensation. It has also been the subject of considerable disagreement concerning its interpretation. Much of the controversy turns on the relevance of this fragment to the famous story that after Archilochos' fellow Parian Lykambes first promised and then denied the warrior-poet his daughter Neoboule in marriage, Archilochos drove both Lykambes and his daughter (daughters in some versions and even wife as well in others) to suicide by hanging. The dishonored and outraged poet supposedly conducted a vendetta in verse publicly denouncing Lykambes as an oath breaker and his daughter(s) as sexually promiscuous that was so vicious it made their lives unbearable. Whatever doubts modern scholars may harbor about the truth of this story, it was taken seriously in antiquity, as witnessed by Kallimachos, inter alios, in a fragment that describes the venom in Archilochos' mouth as being composed of "the dog's pungent bile and the wasp's sharp sting."

Since the fragment, which is in some ways reminiscent of the medieval Provençal *pastorela*, begins with the end of a speech by the young girl who is the object of the speaker's seductive intentions, her identity is crucial to the poem's interpretation. If, as some readers argue, she is Neoboule's sister (though she does not explicitly identify herself as such), then the poet's murderous music may apply to her as well as to her older sister, who is clearly the main target of his degrading verses, making the young girl the physical victim of his desire to belittle and violate the reputation of the house of Lykambes. If, on the other hand, the young girl is taken to be unrelated to the Lykambid Neoboule, though part of her circle, then the poet may be seen to have created a complex little drama in which he successfully balances his malicious desire to degrade the older, whorish girl with a healthy, tender, and self-controlled desire to satisfy himself without defiling the virginal younger one.

I have also consulted the edition of this poem by Merkelbach and West as reprinted by H. D. Rankin, *Archilochus of Paros* (Park Ridge, N.J.: Noyes Press, 1977), pp. 69–71, as well as Anne Pippin Burnett, *Three Archaic Poets: Archilochus, Alcaeus, Sappho* (Cambridge: Harvard University Press, 1983), pp. 84–87. Both of these scholars offer rich and full treatments of the fragment and its critical reception.

"Amphimedo," the name of the young girl's mother, is unique and does not appear in any of the ancient Archilochian *testimonia*. Barring the serendipitous discovery of another, complementary, piece of mummy wrapping, we have no way of knowing if the missing part of the girl's speech clarified the relationship between herself and Neoboule and, thus, if Amphimedo was also the older girl's mother—though that would make it hard to explain the poet's apparent respect for the deceased woman's person. We can only assume what the poem tells us: namely, that the girl has some kind of association with Neoboule and that she recommends the older girl to her ardent lover.

The poet's reference to the "proverb's bitch" alludes to the fable of the sow and the bitch who quarreled about their respective fecundity. When the bitch tried to save her case by pointing out the speed of her delivery, the sow trumped that argument by pointing out that her puppies are born blind.

It should come as no surprise that the fragment's last line has raised the issue of whether the caressed hair in question was on the young girl's head or between her thighs.

I have taken the liberty of changing the verb tense in the poem's final movement from the past to the historical present for the sake of narrative immediacy.

SAPPHO of Mytilene (a city on the island of Lesbos) was born into an aristocratic family and wrote poems that secured her the highest esteem of her fellow Greeks and posterity. As Dioskorides, one of the more important poets in *The Greek Anthology,* said in a panegyric for her, she is to be greeted as a god for having left the world her "immortal daughters, her songs." At one time nine books of poetry were credited to her name, but now we have only some two hundred fragments and just one complete poem. Yet her poetry, the great diversity of translations devoted to it, and the monumental body of scholarly and critical writings about it confirm her high standing among the poets of the world. Though Meleagros writes in the proem to his garland that he has included a few flowers from Sappho, none appear among the amatory poems in Book 5 of the *Anthology,* and the dedicatory epigram under her name in Book 6 is of doubtful ascription, as are the other two epigrams under her name, all of them probably dating from Hellenistic times.

4

I render Sappho's *glukupikron* as "sweet-then-bitter" instead of the customary "bittersweet" out of respect for the Greek's more accurate representation of the all too frequent sequence of love's emotions. The assonance with "invincible" and internal rhyme with "critter" is meant to echo the sound of the original: *glukupikron amachanon orpeton.*

5

This is the only complete poem of Sappho's that has survived. It has been suggested that the shift in Aphrodite's discourse from indirect to direct from the middle of the fifth strophe through the sixth lends a dramatic emphasis to its message of just revenge, and that the ease with which the voice of the goddess coalesces with that of her petitioner may be an effect of the influence on Sappho's poem of contemporary prayers and hymns.

ALKAIOS of Messene, a city in the southwest Peloponnese, should not be confused with the better-known poet and contemporary of Sappho's of the same name from Lesbos. This Alkaios had a fair reputation, especially for his political epigrams.

3

The poet prays for a victory for Peithenor, who was probably set to compete in the Olympic games. "That Trojan boy" (the *Dardanid* in the original) refers to Ganymede, whom Zeus, in the form of an eagle, carried off to Mount Olympos for himself and to serve as cupbearer to the gods. The poets in Book 12 often compare the *eromenos*, or "beloved," to Ganymede, some merely introducing the theme and others expressing fear that Zeus will see their beloved and carry him off, too. See Dioskorides *6*, Kallimachos *10*, Meleagros *33, 38*, Anonymous *4, 17, 18*.

ASKLEPIADES, a native of the island of Samos, was considered one of the most outstanding poets of the Ionian-Alexandrian school. Regarded as highly accomplished and innovative, his poetry influenced that of Dioskorides, Kallimachos, and his two friends and contemporaries Hedylos and Poseidippos, among others. Theokritos refers to him as "Sikelidas" in his *Idyll* 7.39 (ca. 270 B.C.), an alias that was known well enough for Meleagros to use it instead of "Asklepiades" in the proem to his garland.

1

The enchanting girl's name in the original is Didyme. See Philodemos *15* for another reference to the beauty of a dark complexion.

3

The reference to Zeus at the end of the poem is to the story of how he turned himself into a shower of gold and penetrated the brazen chamber in which Danae's father, Akrisios, king of Argos, had confined her. The father had imprisoned his daughter to prevent her from conceiving and giving birth to a son that an oracle had said would kill him. That son was Perseus, who ultimately did cause his grandfather's death.

4

Since poems like Andrew Marvell's "To His Coy Mistress" owe their existence in part to ancient ones like this, I thought I would repay the old Greek poet with a version of his epigram enriched with the seventeenth-century English poet's coinage.

7

Paphos is a city on Cyprus, and its queen, of course, is Aphrodite.

12

Lysidike's woman-on-top specialty, the *keles* (literally, "the racehorse"), was the most expensive ride a hetaira (a high-class prostitute) offered her clients.

15

Asklepiades may be speaking to himself or being addressed by friends at a "symposium," a formal all-male drinking party for aristocrats. This is the first of several poems in this collection that I have translated in the form of a prose poem (see the Translator's Preface).

18

Compare Kallimachos *11*, which was probably inspired by this poem. "Nick" is short for Nikagoras.

19

Philokrates was an unknown poet to whom Asklepiades most likely wished to pay a compliment.

DIOSKORIDES probably lived in the Alexandrian suburb Nikopolis, for a few of his epigrams suggest an Egyptian connection. He was influenced by Asklepiades and Kallimachos, and was himself a model for later poets.

1

The story of Adonis, a beautiful youth Aphrodite was in love with and who was killed by a wild boar, is best known to us through Book 10 of Ovid's *Metamorphoses* and William Shakespeare's great erotic narrative poem *Venus and Adonis,* the most popular of his published works in his day. The celebration of Adonis as a sex and fertility god of rebirth had its roots in Semitic culture, as his Phoenician name, Adon, which means "lord" (compare the Hebrew word *Adonai*), indicates. The death of Adonis was commemorated every summer by grieving women who carried effigies of him and cast them into the sea.

4

One of the best-known stories of the legend of King Midas of Phrygia (he of the golden touch) reveals his preference for the piping of Pan to the harping of Apollo and his consequent punishment by Apollo, who made ass's ears grow out of his head. Midas tried to hide this shame under his headdress. But he could not conceal this abnormality from his barber, who, bursting to expose the secret despite the threat of death, confided it to a hole in the ground. When reeds grew on that spot, and the wind shook through them, they whispered, "Midas has ass's ears." See Book 11 of Ovid's *Metamorphoses.*

HEDYLOS was from the island of Samos, with family connections in Athens. It is recorded that his mother, Hedyle, and maternal grandmother, Moschine, were poets. As mentioned above, he was friendly with Poseidippos and with Asklepiades, who was considerably older. We can infer from one of his poems that he spent some time in Egypt.

1

The stealthy stud Nick, in this "cutting loose" version of mine, is named Nikagoras in the original, and his besotted mark Aggie is Aglaonike. My translation, for all its shifts in diction and playfulness, may be more faithful to the Greek than the Greek boy in it is to the girl. But then, she was a *sympatica* hetaira and it was a *sympotic,* that is, drinking-party, night.

2

I have cast Hedylos' singular use of Love's epithet *lusimeles*, "the limb-loosener," as a kind of birth announcement that explains the causes and effects of overdrinking and overcoming. Love as limb-loosener appears even earlier than Archilochos and Sappho, in Hesiod (fl. 700 B.C.), *Theogony*, 121, 911.

KALLIMACHOS was born in the North African port city of Kyrene and moved as a young man to Alexandria, where he became one of the most important and admired literary figures of his time, exercising a notable influence on Greek and Roman poetry. A respected scholar as well as a prolific writer, he was appointed as chief cataloger of the great Alexandrian library by Ptolemy II Philadelphos. At the height of his celebrity, he engaged in numerous literary debates and was criticized by Asklepiades and Poseidippos, but his most famous quarrel was with his former student and intimate Apollonios of Rhodes, the author of the epic poem *Argonautica* and a bitter rival. In what was to be the most celebrated literary argument of antiquity, Kallimachos sharply attacked long narrative poems in imitation of Homer and favored brief and original lyrical forms, an opposition between him and Apollonios as writers that became personal when Kallimachos was passed over for the job of chief librarian in favor of the younger poet. Though Kallimachos did write some longer poems late in life, they were experimental and episodic rather than plotted along the familiar lines of the cyclic Homeric-style narratives he reviled.

1

The first few words of the first line reflect Kallimachos' position in the literary debate described above. The echoing effect in the last two lines emulates similar wordplay in the original.

3

The lacuna in the second-to-last line probably contained a personal name.

8

Hermes, the divine messenger and patron of land travel, commerce, thieves, guile, and rhetoric, among others things, is invoked here as part of the claim to a piece of good fortune.

9

The very same brutish Cyclops named Polyphemos, who captured and threatened to devour Odysseus along with his small party of men in one of the most famous episodes in Homer's *Odyssey* (Book 9), was daringly recast by Hellenistic poets into a romantic lead who had fallen in love with the sea nymph Galatea. The Philip addressed in the poem is named Philippos in the Greek.

11

The sense of the last line is nicely captured in the English proverb "Set a thief to catch a thief," but the Greeks had no such proverb.

We also have the elegant quatrain in Sir Philip Sidney's sonnet "With How Sad Steps, O Moon," "Sure, if that long-with-love-acquainted eyes / Can judge of love, thou feel'st a lover's case; / I read it in thy looks; thy languished grace, / To me that feel the like, thy state descries."

12

The last line in the original compares the girl to the Megarians, the unfortunate inhabitants of Megara, a city on the Saronic Gulf across from the island of Salamis that had fallen upon hard times. In fact, the oracle at Delphi had tagged Megara with the reputation of being the proverbial "loser" city of Greece, which I have chosen to translate as "ghost town" in my version.

13

This epigram is an example of the *paraclausithyron,* a lover's complaint addressed at his beloved's closed door, which occurs with some frequency in classical poetry. See also Poseidippos 6. One of the best examples of it in English literature is in Geoffrey Chaucer's *Troilus and Criseyde* 5., 540–53, where not only is the door closed, there is nobody home.

MELEAGROS was born in Gadara, Syria, raised in Tyre, and spent most of his life on the island of Kos, northwest of Rhodes off the coast of southwestern Asia Minor. Though famous as the collector of the *Stephanos,* "garland," that provided the nucleus of what was eventually to become *The Greek Anthology,* it is as a poet of remarkable range and originality that he is especially remembered and admired. As some earlier fragments of papyrus suggest, Meleagros may not have been the first individual to collect poems in this fashion, but the size and diversity of his selection gave it special standing. His own poems, which became an important model for later Greek and Roman poets, show how well he knew the work of the Greek poets who had preceded him.

2

Scholars have ascribed this poem and the one that follows it in *The Greek Anthology* to Meleagros as well as to his fellow poet from Gadara, Philodemos (see Philodemos 4). I have split the difference and attributed one poem to each here. Though these two poems differ thematically, Meleagros and his younger contemporary can be quite similar in subject matter as well as stylistically.

6

Pan was the god of flocks and shepherds and originated in Arcadia. Half man and half goat, he had horns, was highly sexed, and invented the reed flute or syrinx, also called the panpipe.

10

The Graces (our word derives from the Latin *Gratiae*), Euphronsyne, Thalia, and Aglaia, were called the *Charites* in Greek, and were goddesses of beauty who influenced the arts.

13

Meleagros satirizes the Hellenistic poetic convention of using an animal to convey a message of love, as in Polyphemos sending dolphins to Galatea. Birds are usually the messengers of choice in world amatory poetry, perhaps the best known being the starling in two poems by the troubadour Marcabru (fl. mid–twelfth century), *Estornel, cueill ta volada* and *Ges l'estornels non s'oblida.*

In the last line, Meleagros compares the tiny insect to Herakles with the reference to the lion pelt and club, the hero's trophies from the first of his twelve legendary labors, the killing of the Nemean lion.

15

The rival lover is a Jew, who maybe also keeps warm with Demo on a chilly Sabbath since he's not allowed to light a fire.

17

The dawn's too early light for lovers is an old and common theme in classical poetry. During the Middle Ages a distinct lyric genre that was possibly rooted in Ovid and other Roman poets developed. The dawn song—*alba* and *aubade* in Provence and northern France, respectively, and *Tagelied* in Germany—enjoyed an unusually popular and, at times, sophisticated currency. Chaucer's serious employment of it in the third book of *Troilus and Criseyde,* his parody of it in the Reeve's Tale, and Shakespeare's dramatic variation on it at the beginning of Act 3, scene 5 of *Romeo and Juliet* are perhaps the best-known examples in English poetry.

Our vocabulary relies on a German word to denote the questionable human feeling of Schadenfreude, but much before the Germans, the Greeks, who always had a word for everything, as the saying goes, had one for this too. To modify the word *phos,* "light," Meleagros uses *epichairekakon,* "that rejoiced at [my] grief."

19

Meleagros introduces the language of the town crier in this poem.

23

Through some ingenious phrasing in the second line of this poem, Meleagros suggests that when she's naked, Kallistion's name should be spelled *Kallischion,* which would then mean "of the beautiful hips" or "flanks."

28

Hides and skins were hung in front of fortifications to screen them from enemy missiles. Nemesis was the goddess of divine retribution.

30

In fact, Love was throwing knucklebones, not dice.

32

Praxiteles "of old" refers to the most important sculptor of the 300s B.C. The new Praxiteles (of "today") refers to a magician who worked with living material rather than stone.

36

This poem is cast as a dialogue between the drunken and the sober selves.

40

At the close of this epigram, Meleagros elicits a double entendre from the word *pamphulo*, combining the meanings of "every race" and "the Pamphylian Sea," which is situated off the western end of Cyprus. "Fire Island" is my parachronistic contribution to the poem's polysemous ending.

NOSSIS was from the city of Lokroi, on the southeastern coast of the Italian boot's toe. She is the only woman poet represented in Book 5, though Meleagros included her and several other women in his garland. Meleagros must have known other love poems by her, for in his proem he writes, "Love melted the wax on her writing tablets." The different endings of my two versions reflect the divided state of the textual emendations of the poem's last line.

PLATO, the great philosopher and founder of the Academy, was thought to have written poetry as a young man and is represented by a number of epigrams in *The Greek Anthology.* While some of these poems are well attested, Platonic authorship is a fairly vexed question.

1

This most famous of *testimonia* to the life and works of Sappho appears in Book 9 and is not an amatory epigram, though it clearly expresses love for her poetry if not her person. See *Phaedrus* 325c, where Plato refers to her as "lovely Sappho."

2, 3

Both of these poems are in the persona of Socrates. Platonic authorship of Poem *3* has been challenged, and ascription to Philodemos has even been proposed, but that is not without its own problems. Xanthippe was Socrates' wife.

4

This poem from Book 6, *Anathematica* ("Dedicatory Epigrams") has been attributed either to Pseudo-Plato or Anonymous. By opting for the former, I include the poem here. Laïs was both notorious and famous as the most desirable hetaira of her time.

POSEIDIPPOS, a native of Pella in Macedonia, was friends with Hedylos and the older Asklepiades. For a very long time, he was known as the author of about twenty-three poems, but that changed in the early 1990s when what has turned out to be one of the most exciting recent discoveries in classical literature was made in the cartonnage of a mummy dating from around 170 B.C., a papyrus roll of some 112 epigrams. Presumably, all of the poems in this singular collection, acquired by the University of Milan, where it was preserved, edited, and published, are by Poseidippos—two of them are copies of already extant poems ascribed to him in antiquity. The epigrams in "the Milan papyrus," however, are didactic, not a single one erotic, and thus it is not a comprehensive collection of his work.

1

Zeno and Kleanthes were both heads of the Stoic school. Swans were believed to sing sweetly and their plumage suggested venerable age, so Zeno, who was not a poet, is described as a "learned swan" on the strength of his philosophical writings. The younger Kleanthes was a poet, but his Muse was considered to be the inspiration of all his writings.

5

This poem on behalf of the obliging hetaira Kallistion seems out of place in Book 12. The islands of Kypros and Kythera were traditionally associated with Aphrodite. Miletos was an important city on the southwestern coast of Asia Minor.

6

Addressed to the door of Pythias' house, this poem is another example of *paraclausithyron.*

RHIANOS, it is likely, was originally a slave from Crete. Ancient sources tell us he wrote epic poems and edited Homer, as well as composing a number of epigrams. The Hours were the daughters of Zeus and Themis, the goddess of law, and were goddesses of nature and order who also made gifts of beauty.

ANTIPHILOS of Byzantium was a contemporary of Philippos of Thessalonika's. This poem describes a picture of the well-known myth in which

Zeus changed into a swan in order to mate with Leda, the wife of the Spartan king Tyndareus. The most common version of the result of this union reported the birth of two sets of twins, Helen of Troy and Klytemnestra, and the Dioscuri, Kastor and Polydeukes, all of whom had important destinies. Laconia was the local territory of Sparta and the Eurotas its major river. In the original, the bird of the last word is a "crested lark," which was considered comical in antiquity.

AUTOMEDON probably lived during the Augustan era, 27 B.C. to A.D. 14, but we have no firm dates for him or information about his life.

BASSUS may have been the Lollius Bassus who has several poems in *The Greek Anthology.* Other than an educated guess that he was born in Smyrna, we know nothing about him. The girl in this poem is named Korinna and her price is two obols.

DIODOROS may have been one of a couple of Diodoroses—one of Tarsos, another known as Zonas—who are represented in the *Anthology.* Though this poem appears in Book 5, its subject suggests it belongs in Book 12. See the note on Straton below.

KRINAGORAS, of Mytilene on the island of Lesbos, served as an ambassador to Julius Caesar in Rome and to Augustus Caesar in Spain.

MACCIUS bears an Italian family name.

MARCUS ARGENTARIUS, one of the Greco-Roman epigrammatists, was also a rhetorician of some reputation. His life spanned the end of the first century B.C. and the beginning of the first century A.D.

1
Melissa means "honeybee" in Greek.

9

This poem is not from Book 5, the *Erotica Epigrammata,* but from Book 9, *Epideictica,* poems of blame and praise. In keeping with the tradition in which *The Greek Anthology* was shaped, I have moved around a few poems for the sake of my own garland.

PHILODEMOS was born in Gadara, Syria, studied with Zeno in Athens, and taught at the Epicurean School in Naples, where Horace and Virgil attended his lectures. It is likely that he knew Catullus, whose work he appears to have influenced as well. Although Vesuvius' biggest blast covered the estate, in Herculaneum near Pompeii, of his chief patron, L. Calpurnius Piso Caesoninus, under ash and lava, many of the papyrus rolls that survived are of his works on various topics. Philodemos was one of the earliest advocates of art for art's sake, rejecting contemporary utilitarian theories and arguing against the separation of form and content. It is thought Meleagros was not aware of his compatriot's writing; otherwise he surely would have included some of it in his garland. Fortunately, Philippos collected a number of his poems for his anthology, for the twenty-nine poems that have been ascribed with certainty to Philodemos are considered among the finest in *The Greek Anthology.*

2

Grace is "Charito" in the original.

5

This is one of a number of poems that inappropriately ended up in Book 12 of *The Greek Anthology* as a result of a misunderstanding of the gender of diminutives like "Thermion" in the first line and "Demarion" in the fifth, which I have translated as "little . . . Demo." Most editors do not blame Straton for this "blunder" but some Byzantine, even Konstantinos Kephalas himself.

6

I have translated the original's "Ionian Sea" as "Lake Michigan" because the former, though unexceptional to an ancient audience, is not so to us, while the latter directs us to a recognizable geographical commonplace.

Flo in the Greek is "Naias," which some insist, quite correctly if unnecessarily, is a girl's name and not that of the water nymph.

7
Find the line indebted to Dylan Thomas.

9, 16
Each of these poems is spoken by a woman.

11
Endymion was beloved by Selene (the Moon), who asked Zeus to grant him one wish. Endymion chose eternal sleep and fell asleep as a beautiful young man forever.

15
Andromeda, an Ethiopian princess, was rescued and married by Perseus, the son of Zeus and Danae, when he saw her tied to a rock as a sacrificial victim in expiation of her mother's imprudent and impudent boast that she, Kassiopeia, was more beautiful than all the Nereids (sea goddesses) put together. The actual area of India was not always well defined.

17
This poem is from Book 9, containing epideictic and ecphrastic epigrams. Editors disagree about the authenticity of a closing couplet in the voice of Xantho: "Don't you get it, man, you loan officer, / you'll live forever in a stone-cut single bed, creep." I have done my best here with the insults—*tokogluphos*, one who keeps close track of his interest, and *dusmorphe*, misshapen or ill-favored one—but I finally agree with those who reject this alleged lesson on how to be a better Epicurean as part of Philodemos' poem.

18–20
These three poems are from Book 11, which contains the convivial and satirical epigrams. I have included these, along with Poem *17*, because of their amatory implications. The reference to Mytilene in Poem *19* is to the major city on the island of Lesbos.

AGATHIAS SCHOLASTIKOS of Myrina, a city on the western coast of Asia Minor, studied law in Alexandria and Constantinople (see his Poem *3*). He made the collection of contemporary poems known as *The Cycle of Agathias Scholastikos*, which he says he presented in Constantinople to Theodoros, son of Kosmas. As his title *"scholastikos"* suggests, he was a highly respected literary figure.

2

Pittalakos was a notorious individual whose bad moral character was attacked by Aeschines (ca. 400–320 B.C.), an Athenian orator and a resolute enemy of Demosthenes'. The reference is indicative of Agathias' learned style and implies the exclusively literary nature of this poetic exercise.

LEONTIOS may have been the *referendarius,* an official who dealt with petitions and requests, in the court of Emperor Justinian that Procopius of Caesarea (fl. A.D. 550) mentions in his *Secret History.* If he was, he came from Cilicia, on the coast of Asia Minor across from Cyprus, gave and took bribes (on a rather large scale), influenced the emperor to do likewise, had a reputation for perverting justice and being extraordinarily devoted to the love of money—and still had time to write poetry, though Procopius does not mention it as one of his activities.

MAKEDONIOS HYPATOS (Macedonius the Consul) has more than forty poems in the *Anthology,* about half of which are in Book 5.

6

The lady's name in Greek is Parmenis, which is related to the word *parameno,* "to stand by" or "to stand fast," i.e., to be constant.

PALLADAS was an Alexandrian teacher of literature who has more than 150 poems in *The Greek Anthology.* This poem is one of three that appear in Book 5. Zeus came to Europa, Leda, and Danae as a bull, a swan, and a golden shower, respectively.

PAULOS SILENTIARIUS was a man of prominence during the reign of Justinian. In addition to maintaining order and silence in the imperial court, the *silentiarius* could also be a confidential adviser. He wrote a long poem, *Description of the Church of Hagia Sophia,* in addition to his numerous epigrams, which have earned him the high regard of scholars and critics. He was a close friend to Agathias Scholastikos, who was married to his daughter.

1

In his reply to Agathias' letter (see his Poem *3*), Paulos makes a humorous comparison between his friend and the legendary lover Leandros. He and his beloved, Hero, lived in towns on the opposites sides of the Hellespont, and the young man from Abydos swam every night across the water to Sestos, guided by a light Hero placed in a high tower. One night the lamp was extinguished during a storm and the lover lost his way and drowned, causing his beloved to throw herself from her tower after she discovered his body. In 1598, Christopher Marlowe began to write his version of the story, the unfinished poem *Hero and Leander*, which George Chapman, a poet and translator of Homer, completed.

2

Semiramis was a Babylonian queen who built herself a great city on the banks of the Euphrates that was surrounded by a wall of legendary dimensions.

The last line may suggest that Paulos followed his job description in his private as well as his public affairs.

3

On Zeus and Danae, see the note above on Poem *3* by Asklepiades.

7, 8

Tantalos appears near the end of Book 11 (582ff.) of Homer's *Odyssey*, "The Kingdom of the Dead," where, for offending the gods, he is punished with eternal thirst and hunger by being set up to his neck in a pool of water under a branch heavy with fruit; when he bends to drink, the water recedes, and when he raises his arm to pick a fruit, the tree branch springs out of reach. In the second half of Poem *7*, Paulos refers to yet another punishment inflicted upon Tantalos, the placement above his head of an enormous stone that seems on the verge of falling but always remains balanced (see Pindar, *Olympian* 1.55ff.). Our word "tantalize" derives from his name.

Rufinus Domesticus has one poem in *The Greek Anthology* by virtue of its inclusion in *The Cycle of Agathias Scholastikos.*

Archias is the name of three different poets in *The Greek Anthology*. The only thing we know about this one is that he probably lived during the late first century B.C.

2
The word *Kypris* was commonly used to denote Aphrodite from Alexandrian times on. The reference is to the island of Cyprus, the mythical birthplace of love's goddess. I have generally retained its Greek form, although on some occasions, as here, I translate it as "Goddess." Note that in this poem she has taken up archery, an activity generally associated with her son Eros.

Capito is a Roman cognomen.

Dionysios Sophistes is the name heading this epigram in Book 5. We know nothing more about him.

Diophanes of Myrina is the author of the last poem in Book 5.

Gallus is another poet about whom we know nothing.

Killaktor, if he is the same as Kallikter of Manesium in other references, lived during the late first century A.D. The last word in the poem, *phusios,* means "nature" and was used as a term for the sexual organs.

Nikarchos lived in Alexandria. This poem, addressed to Similos, is in Book 5.

NOUMENIOS OF TARSOS, a major city of Cilicia in Asia Minor, leaves no record other than this epigram. In the original, the name Kyros at the beginning of the poem plays on the Greek word for "lord," *kyrios.*

RUFINUS, for whom we have no firm dates, must have lived sometime between A.D. 150 and 400. Because the first hundred or so poems in Book 5 of *The Greek Anthology* contain thirty-six poems by Rufinus and no work of his appears elsewhere in the entire *Anthology,* scholars have assumed that the poet had made his own anthology, in which he included his own poems as well as a good number from *The Garland of Meleagros.* This grouping was then combined with those from Meleagros, Philippos, and Agathias by later Byzantine hands to arrange the final presentation of Book 5 as it now stands.

1

The form of this first of the Rufinian poems as a tourist's letter from the great Ionian city of Ephesos in Asia Minor has been taken as a clue that he came from someplace fairly nearby. This is the only epigram in which Rufinus mentions himself by name.

Like her twin, Apollo, Artemis was the child of Zeus and Leto, and was worshipped as an eternally young virgin goddess of the wild, the hunt, and childbirth. Her temple in Ephesos, where her veneration was integrated with the cult of the Asiatic mother-goddess Kybele, was counted as one of the Seven Wonders of the World.

4

Praxiteles (300s B.C.) and Polykleitos (late 400s B.C.) were among the most important sculptors of their times.

5

The rhetorical device Rufinus uses in the closing couplet to magnify by comparison the event set forth in the lines that precede it was known as "the impossibility," *adynaton* (*adynata,* plural).

6, 9

In both of these poems, Rufinus imagines himself enacting a parody of the famous Judgment of Paris on Mount Ida, in which the young Trojan prince was forced to decide which of three goddesses—Aphrodite, Athena, or Hera—was the most beautiful.

The two-line lacuna in the middle of Poem *6* is unusual for a poem in the *Anthology*.

7

Boopie in the original is "Boöpis."

8

In the fourth and sixth lines, the words *spatale* (bracelets) and *spatalon* (wanton) play off against each other, an effect I've tried to approximate with "gold . . . bracelets" and "brazen."

12

Some scholars believe that this poem might be by Asklepiades.

15

Amy in the original is "Amymone."

20

Hecuba was the second wife of King Priam of Troy and bore him fifteen children, the most famous of which were Hector, Paris, Cassandra, and Troilus. It was during the reign of this aged royal couple that the city of Troy fell to the Greeks. I have retained the traditional spellings of these names.

SKYTHINOS was probably a contemporary of Straton's.

STRATON of Sardis, an inland city of Asia Minor, lived during the reign of Emperor Hadrian. He is famous as the compiler of an anthology of homoerotic epigrams titled *Mousa Paidike* ("Pederastic Poems"), as it is called by Konstantinos Kephalas in his preface to Book 12 of *The Greek Anthology*. Some scholars believe that the ninety-six poems by Straton that occur in Book 12 constitute the whole of his original anthology, while others believe he added selections from the garlands of Meleagros, Philippos, and other minor sources. It is unlikely that Straton was responsible for the inclusion of a number of heterosexual poems in this collection; the most reasonable explanation for the state of Book 12 as it has come down to us is that Straton's original anthology was amplified and rearranged by the Byzantine Kephalas.

1

The first two "dicknames," *lalou* and *koko,* come directly from the Greek. In the last line, Straton puns on the Greek for "you'll know" (*oidas*) and the word for "to swell" or "swollen" (*oideo*). (Note that in Sophocles' tragedy *Oedipus Rex* the meaning of the hero's name is "swollen foot.") Literally, the line reads, "As for the more perfect one, you know what you should call it." I use the word "swellest" in my last line to convey the sense of that wordplay.

3

The letters of the Greek alphabet were used to denote numbers. The sum of the numerical values of the letters in each of these words in Greek is 1,570.

5

I have changed the point of view in this poem from the first person to the third as a way of evoking the poem "He Asked About the Quality" by the twentieth-century Alexandrian Greek poet C. P. Cavafy.

7

Astyanax was the baby boy of Hector and Andromache of Troy. After his father's death and the fall of the city, the attacking Greeks threw Astyanax to his death from the top of a tower.

11

Aphrodite Rising was a famous painting by Apelles (fl. 350–320 B.C.), an important artist and a favorite painter of Alexander the Great's. The love goddess is depicted emerging from the waves and pressing sea foam out of her hair, antiquity's counterpart to *The Birth of Venus* by Sandro Botticelli (1444–1510).

Straton alludes to the Judgment of Paris as part of his poetic agenda to make traditional myth relevant to his kind of love, which he manages to do with a sense of humor.

17

This is one of five epigrams by Straton that appear in Book 11. The poet parodies the famous Homeric formula "the rosy-fingered dawn" to describe a maturing boy's progress.

19

Cy in the original is "Kyris."

ANONYMOUS encompasses the poems presented in this collection without ascription from all periods covered in *The Greek Anthology*. It is possible that some of these epigrams were written by some of the named poets in this anthology but lost their attributions over time. The high incidence of anonymous epigrams in Book 12 is probably the result of Meleagros' incorporation into his garland of erotic poems that derived from a pederastic collection that did not name authors.

10

The "love charm" Niko dedicates to Aphrodite has been explained as a disk, or wheel, which is made to revolve in one and then the opposite direction through the manipulation of rotating strings. Niko's home city, Larissa, is in Thessaly, a place reputed in antiquity for its sorceresses because of its magic herbs.

14

The picture given is of a statue carved in wood except for the extremities, which were done in marble or stone, a common technique.

15, 16

Knidos was a prosperous city on the southwestern coast of Asia Minor. The marble statue there of a naked Aphrodite by Praxiteles (ca. 364 B.C.) was considered the most beautiful sculpture in the world. It was generally believed that its model was the beautiful hetaira Phryne, and some of its admirers had to be restrained from passionately embracing it. According to these epigrams, the young man with the Persian-sounding name, Aribazos, was another attraction around town.

17

Check "Leda and the Swan" by William Butler Yeats for echoes.

19

Myrtle berries were used to flavor wine and as a condiment in cooking, much like pepper. Some berries would have been strewn on the floor, along with other scraps, after a symposium. For "Graces," see the note above on Poem *10* by Meleagros.

20

The young fighter's name means "staunch in battle" in Greek. Long woolen fillets were tied around the head and limbs of victorious athletes. Myrrh runs from trees, just as blood does from wounds, but it was also used in unguents. For a modern poem with a similar climactic kiss, see C. P. Cavafy's "The Bandaged Shoulder" (1919).

LIST OF SOURCES FOR THE
ORIGINAL GREEK

Sources for all of the poems in this anthology may be conveniently found in the four editions cited below. The italicized numbers refer to the poems in this collection; the numbers following the hyphens identify the items as enumerated in the sources. Immediately following the first three poets, the names of the poets from *The Greek Anthology* have been listed in strict alphabetical order rather than by the sequence of their appearance in this book.

David A. Campbell. *Greek Lyric Poetry*. Vol. 1. Loeb Classical Library. Cambridge: Harvard University Press, 1990.

J. M. Edmonds. *Lyra Graeca*. Vol. 2. Loeb Classical Library. Revised and augmented edition. Cambridge: Harvard University Press, 1952.

Douglas E. Gerber. *Greek Iambic Poetry*. Loeb Classical Library. Cambridge: Harvard University Press, 1999.

W. R. Paton. *The Greek Anthology*. 5 vols. Loeb Classical Library. Cambridge: Harvard University Press, 1916; reprinted 1999.

I have also consulted Eva-Marie Voigt, *Sappho et Alcaeus: Fragmenta* (Amsterdam: Athenaeum-Polak and Van Gennep, 1971); A.S.F. Gow and D. L. Page, *The Greek Anthology: Hellenistic Epigrams*, 2 vols. (Cambridge, England: Cambridge University Press, 1965); Gow and Page, *The Greek Anthology: The Garland of Philip and Some Contemporary Epigrams*, 2 vols. (Cambridge, England: Cambridge University Press, 1968); and David Sider, *The Epigrams of Philodemos* (New York: Oxford University Press, 1997).

ANAKREON
Edmonds, *Lyra Graeca*
1-2, p. 138, and 11, p. 142; *2*-3, p. 138; *3*-4, p. 138; *4*-21, p. 148; *5*-31, p. 154;
6-48, p. 162; *7*-75, p. 176; *8*-101, p. 190; *9*-84, p. 180; *10*-104, p. 192; *11*-15,
pp. 144, 146; *12*-25, p. 150

ARCHILOCHOS
Gerber, *Greek Iambic Poetry*
1-30, 31, p. 104; *2*-191, p. 204; *3*-196, p. 210; *4*-331, p. 292; *5*-42, p. 112; *6*-196a,
pp. 210, 212, 214

SAPPHO
Campbell, *Greek Lyric Poetry*
1-33, p. 82; *2*-47, p. 92; *3*-102, p. 126; *4*-130, p. 146; *5*-1, pp. 52, 54

POETS FROM *THE GREEK ANTHOLOGY*

Paton, *The Greek Anthology*. All references following the italicized numbers are
to book and poem numbers in *The Greek Anthology*.

AGATHIAS SCHOLASTIKOS
1-5.261, *2*-5.278, *3*-5.292

ALKAIOS
1-5.10, *2*-12.30, *3*-12.64

ANONYMOUS
1-5.2, *2*-5.50, *3*-5.51, *4*-5.65, *5*-5.83, *6*-5.84, *7*-5.91, *8*-5.99, *9*-5.101, *10*-5.205,
11-5.304, *12*-12.17, *13*-12.19, *14*-12.40, *15*-12.61, *16*-12.62, *17*-12.67, *18*-12.69,
19-12.107, *20*-12.123, *21*-12.136, *22*-12.151

ANTIPHILOS
5.307

ARCHIAS
1-5.59, *2*-5.98

ASKLEPIADES
1-5.210, *2*-5.7, *3*-5.64, *4*-5.85, *5*-5.145, *6*-5.153, *7*-5.158, *8*-5.162, *9*-5.169, *10*-5.185, *11*-5.189, *12*-5.203, *13*-5.207, *14*-12.46, *15*-12.50, *16*-12.75, *17*-12.105, *18*-12.135, *19*-12.162, *20*-12.166

AUTOMEDON
1-12.34, *2*-5.129

BASSUS
5.125

CAPITO
5.67

DIODOROS
5.122

DIONYSIOS SOPHISTES
5.81

DIOPHANES OF MYRINA
5.309

DIOSKORIDES
1-5.53, *2*-5.54, *3*-5.55, *4*-5.56, *5*-12.14, *6*-12.37, *7*-12.42, *8*-12.170

GALLUS
5.49

HEDYLOS
1-5.199, *2*-11.414

KALLIMACHOS
1-12.43, *2*-12.71, *3*-12.73, *4*-12.102, *5*-12.118, *6*-12.139, *7*-12.148, *8*-12.149, *9*-12.150, *10*-12.230, *11*-12.134, *12*-5.6, *13*-5.23

KILLAKTOR
5.45

KRINAGORAS
5.119

LEONTIOS
5.295

MACCIUS
5.133

MAKEDONIOS HYPATOS
1-5.233, *2*-5.224, *3*-5.231, *4*-5.240, *5*-5.243, *6*-5.247

MARCUS ARGENTARIUS
1-5.32, *2*-5.89, *3*-5.102, *4*-5.104, *5*-5.110, *6*-5.113, *7*-5.116, *8*-5.127, *9*-9.554

MELEAGROS
1-5.8, *2*-5.24, *3*-5.57, *4*-5.96, *5*-5.136, *6*-5.139, *7*-5.141, *8*-5.143, *9*-5.144, *10*-5.149, *11*-5.157, *12*-5.151, *13*-5.152, *14*-5.156, *15*-5.160, *16*-5.163, *17*-5.173, *18*-5.175, *19*-5.177, *20*-5.180, *21*-5.184, *22*-5.191, *23*-5.192, *24*-5.197, *25*-5.204, *26*-5.208, *27*-5.215, *28*-12.33, *29*-12.41, *30*-12.47, *31*-12.60, *32*-12.57, *33*-12.70, *34*-12.81, *35*-12.82, *36*-12.117, *37*-12.132, *38*-12.133, *39*-12.147, *40*-12.157, *41*-12.164, *42*-12.86

NIKARCHOS
5.38

NOSSIS
5.170

NOUMENIOS OF TARSOS
12.28

PALLADAS
5.257

PAULOS SILENTIARIUS
1-5.293, *2*-5.252, *3*-5.217, *4*-5.219, *5*-5.230, *6*-5.232, *7*-5.236, *8*-5.246, *9*-5.266

PHILODEMOS
1-5.4, *2*-5.13, *3*-5.46, *4*-5.25, *5*-12.173, *6*-5.107, *7*-5.112, *8*-5.115, *9*-5.120, *10*-5.121, *11*-5.123, *12*-5.124, *13*-5.126, *14*-5.131, *15*-5.132, *16*-5.306, *17*-9.570, *18*-11.30, *19*-11.34, *20*-11.41

PLATO
1-9.506, *2*-5.78, *3*-5.80, *4*-6.1

POSEIDIPPOS
1-5.134, *2*-5.186, *3*-12.45, *4*-12.120, *5*-12.131, *6*-5.213, *7*-5.211

RHIANOS
12.38

RUFINUS
1-5.9, *2*-5.12, *3*-5.14, *4*-5.15, *5*-5.19, *6*-5.36, *7*-5.22, *8*-5.27, *9*-5.35, *10*-5.41, *11*-5.42, *12*-5.44, *13*-5.47, *14*-5.66, *15*-5.73, *16*-5.77, *17*-5.87, *18*-5.88, *19*-5.92, *20*-5.103

RUFINUS DOMESTICUS
5.284

SKYTHINOS
1-12.22, *2*-12.232

STRATON
1-12.3, *2*-12.5, *3*-12.6, *4*-12.7, *5*-12.8, *6*-12.9, *7*-12.11, *8*-12.192, *9*-12.176, *10*-12.185, *11*-12.207, *12*-12.210, *13*-12.205, *14*-12.211, *15*-12.216, *16*-12.222, *17*-11.21, *18*-12.236, *19*-12.213, *20*-12.240, *21*-12.248

ABOUT THE TRANSLATOR

GEORGE ECONOMOU graduated from Colgate University and received his M.A. and Ph.D. from Columbia University. Professor emeritus of English at the University of Oklahoma, he is the author of seven books of poetry, most recently *Century Dead Center*, and numerous translations from ancient and modern Greek. A critic and scholar of medieval literature, he has translated William Langland's *Piers Plowman* and written and edited several books including *The Goddess Natura in Medieval Literature*. He is the recipient of numerous fellowships from the National Endowment for the Arts and the Rockefeller Foundation.

A NOTE ON THE TYPE

The principal text of this Modern Library edition
was set in a digitized version of Janson, a typeface that
dates from about 1690 and was cut by Nicholas Kis,
a Hungarian working in Amsterdam. The original matrices have
survived and are held by the Stempel foundry in Germany.
Hermann Zapf redesigned some of the weights and sizes for
Stempel, basing his revisions on the original design.